Green parenting

About the author

Melissa Corkhill, writer, mother of two and editor of The Green Parent magazine is passionate about natural parenting and green issues.

With a background in media, Melissa launched the UKs fastest-growing green lifestyle magazine four years ago. She now co-creates it with her partner whilst home-educating their two children. They live in a village in East Sussex along with chickens and a menagerie of other wildlife.

Melissa believes in raising awareness so that parents can make informed choices about their family's health and wellbeing. Her work has been described as "inspiring, strong and beautiful"

I dedicate this book to to my family

Green parenting

The best for you, your children and the environment

Green parenting
ISBN 1 904601 39 1

First published in Great Britain in 2006 by Impact Publishing Ltd.
12 Pierrepont Street, Bath, BA1 1LA
info@impactpublishing.co.uk
www.impactpublishing.co.uk

All rights reserved. No reproduction, copy or transmission of this publication may be made without written permission. No paragraph of this publication may be reproduced, copied or transmitted save with written permission or in accordance with the provisions of the Copyright Act 1956 (as amended). Any person who does any unauthorised act in relation to this publication may be liable to criminal prosecution and civil claims for damages.

Neither the Publishers nor the Author can accept liability for the use of the materials or methods recommended in this book or for any consequences arising out of their use, nor can they be held responsible for any errors or omissions that may be found in the text or may occur at a future date as a result of changes in rules, laws or equipment.

© 2006 by Melissa Corkhill.

Melissa Corkhill is hereby identified as the author of this work in accordance with section 77 of the Copyright Designs and Patent Act 1988.

A Cataloguing in Publication record for this title is available from the British Library.

Credits: Photo credits; the Green Parent magazine.

Printed and bound in the UK by PIMS Print Crewkerne.

CONTENTS

Introduction 7-8

Chapter 1: Natural Pregnancy and Birth 9-28
Fertility 10-11
Infertility 11
Natural pregnancy 12
A month-by-month guide to pregnancy 13
Natural treatments during pregnancy 18-20
Common problems and how to treat them 21-24
Birth 25-26
Looking after yourself after the birth 27-28

Chapter 2: Natural Babies 29-42
Breastfeeding 30-32
Common breastfeeding problems and how to treat them 33-34
Holistic bottlefeeding if you can't breastfeed 35
Weaning 36
Baby massage 37
Baby wearing 38
Real Nappies 39-41
Other eco-friendly alternatives 41

Chapter 3: Green Nutrition 43-64
Food Miles 44-45
Additives 45-47
Genetically modified foods 48
Organic food 49-53
Vegetarianism 53
Nutrition for the family 54-55
Recipes 56-61
Grow your own 62-64

Green parenting

Chapter 4: Holistic Health 65-80
Alternative medicine chest 67
Holistic therapies 68-70
Ways to de-stress 70
The importance of exercise 71-72
Common childhood ailments and ways to treat them 73-76
Immunity and Vaccinations 77-80

Chapter 5: Green Education 81-96
Teaching children about the environment 82
Fun green activities for families 83-86
Green toys 87
The effect of TV 88-90
Alternative education 91-92
A day in the life of a home educating family 93-96

Chapter 6: The Natural Home 97-112
The alternatives 98-100
A guide to chemicals in the home 101-103
What to use for a naturally clean home 104
A natural home 105-107
Energy conservation 108
Organic gardening 109
How to create an eco-friendly garden 110-111
Gardening with kids 112

50 Ways to be a green parent 113-118

Contacts and Resources 119-125

Introduction

Being a green parent is about more than demonstrating respect for the planet and raising your children to be aware of environmental issues. Green parenting is primarily about raising your children with love and respect. It's about listening to them and nurturing them in the hope that they will grow up to be healthy individuals who are compassionate about others and our world.

We have pillaged the earth of its natural resources for centuries. Every minute, 26 hectares of rainforest are cut down. That is an area equivalent to 37 football pitches, every sixty seconds. As a result of global warming, as many as half a million species of plants and animals could become extinct by the year 2050. Over twenty-four countries around the world are currently fighting a war; that's over twelve percent of the world's nations involved in conflict. Governments appear to be blinkered about the destruction being inflicted upon our natural environment on a daily basis.

But amid all this doom and gloom, amid all this devastation, there is a ray of hope, a shift in consciousness. The green movement has been growing in number and power since the 1970s when the first CND marches took place in protest against nuclear weapons, when vegetarian and veganism became more widely accepted and when the term 'organic' began to be used to describe farming methods. Thirty or so years later, three quarters of UK households now choose some organic foods and millions of us believe in peace and strongly

Green parenting

oppose war. We are changing organically. Over one third of us now use alternative therapies to treat our families when sick. More and more children are cycling or walking to school rather than travelling by car because it's better for our health and the environment. And, 15% of us realise the environmental impact of using disposable nappies and have chosen the only viable option for the future of our planet, the cotton washable nappy.

This positive change is vital to the survival of our environment and therefore, to the future of our children. If we can do one thing to better our lives today and improve our future for tomorrow it is to go green.

Change can start off small. Stop throwing cans in the bin and start recycling them. Leave the car at home and walk to school instead. Switch off the TV and play a board game. If children are raised in a household that cares about the environment, they will grow up confident in the knowledge that small changes can make a difference. This will have a ripple effect as more and more families and young people start becoming more eco-aware. This book offers information and inspiration about going green from bumps to birth and beyond and shows how it will benefit you, your family and the planet.

1

Natural pregnancy and birth

Green parenting

Pregnancy is the start of the parenting journey. It is an incredible period of creativity and change during which it is important to nurture both body and mind. A woman's body is often optimally healthy during pregnancy and this state of health can be encouraged through a good diet and holistic therapies. There are natural ways to approach birth that work in harmony with the mother's body and encourage the best possible experience for the baby and the labouring woman.

Natural fertility

So, you have decided that you would like to have a baby. Here are some ways to increase your fertility naturally.

What to do if you are planning a baby

- **Choose organic.** Build up yours and your partner's health by eating an organic wholefood diet
- **Consult a nutritionist or a naturopath**
- **Get adequate exercise** and make time for deep relaxation
- **Green your home** and immediate environment. Avoid toxic chemicals wherever possible
- **Read and get hold of as much information** about pregnancy and parenting as possible. Look for inspirational material that is in tune with your ethics
- **Talk to others** about their parenting experiences. Build a support group of like-minded people

What is a Pre-conception Plan?

Many experts recommend a four to six month plan for mothers and fathers before having a baby. This helps the body to eliminate accumulated toxins and get into the best possible state of health. The Foresight Plan is one such programme based mainly on a series of nutritional tests and a tailored organic diet.

Infertility

Many couples find that it takes six months or longer to get pregnant. If you have had unprotected sex for over a year without conceiving, you will be diagnosed as having fertility problems. However, the most important advice is not to panic. An increasing number of fertility problems are stress-related. Other factors include age (fertility decreases in women over 35), hormonal problems and past methods of contraception. In men, common causes of infertility are smoking, alcohol consumption, obesity and stress. In recent years there has been concern over falling sperm counts, which have been linked to plastics, pesticides and hormones in our water supply. In the last 12 years men's sperm counts may have fallen by as much as 29 percent according to a study by the Aberdeen Fertility Centre. In order to avoid these potential hazards, it is best to follow an organic diet and avoid exposure to toxic chemicals in the home. German research has shown a link between disposable nappies and a low sperm count in young boys. You can choose to use cotton real nappies which allow the baby to regulate his own temperature and do not present the same risks.

What to do if you have problems conceiving

- The best position for conception is missionary with the man on top. Women should lie still for 20 minutes after ejaculation

- Avoid cigarettes and caffeine, as these can interfere with sperm production

- Make sure that you both get time to relax. Take up a sport or hobby. Try yoga or meditation

- Diet is important. Eat plenty of wholefoods, especially foods rich in zinc and EFAs (essential fatty acids). Good sources are nuts and seeds. Many cold pressed oils such as argan oil (www.wildwoodgroves.com), hemp seed oil (www.yaoh.co.uk) and flax seed oil, contain high levels of EFAs and can be used to create a delicious nutty salad dressing

- Seek the advice of a herbalist or nutritionist.

Green parenting

Natural pregnancy

Pregnancy is, truly, a miraculous event. Eating well and looking after your body will protect you and your baby during pregnancy, birth and beyond.

It is important not to treat pregnancy as an illness. Carrying on with everyday life and getting daily exercise can help to ensure an easier birth as your body will be more supple and the muscles more able to support your body during childbirth.

Many women feel anxious at the thought of birth. In our society, we often live far from family members and birth wisdom is not often passed down through the generations as it is in tribal cultures. It is a good idea to talk to other women, your partner or a supportive group. They should be people with whom you can share not only your fears, but also your hopes and aspirations for the birth. A good place to access this sort of support is through an active birth class where you can also learn yoga techniques to help your body open up for birth.

Signs of pregnancy

Many women just 'know' that they are pregnant. Some feel different as soon as conception takes place. However, some of the more obvious physical effects of early pregnancy are:

- Missing a period
- Tender or swollen breasts
- Nausea, especially first thing in the morning
- Tiredness
- More frequent trips to the toilet
- Loss of appetite or cravings
- Heightened senses.

A month-by-month guide to pregnancy

Month One

Your Baby An embryo is formed that is between ¼ to ½ an inch long, the size of half a pea. The heart is usually beating by the 25th day.

You As well as the signs already mentioned, you might have an aversion to things you normally enjoy, like coffee or onions and you'll also need to urinate more often.

Month Two

Your Baby By the end of the second month, she resembles a human with a nervous system, organs, eyes, ears and limb buds.

You Your ligaments are beginning to soften, your sense of smell may be heightened and your skin may feel more sensitive. The early stages can be very tiring and you may find yourself needing more rest.

Month Three

Your Baby The foetus can roll, somersault, swallow and is developing its sucking reflex. Her organs are now functional and she has downy hair all over her body.

You As the amount of blood in your body continues to increase (by the end of pregnancy you will have almost 50 percent more than you did before you became pregnant) you may find your temperature rising. Nausea tends to stop around the end of the third month, but heartburn can become a problem.

Green parenting

A month-by-month guide to pregnancy

Month Four

Your Baby   She hears her first sounds. Her unique fingerprints have formed on her fingertips. They are as long as an adult hand.

You   You now have a visible bump. You may notice skin changes such as darkening of freckles and moles. Your hair will probably appear glossier and thicker.

Month Five

Your Baby   Her bones are beginning to harden. She can now grasp hold of the umbilical cord.

You   You may start to feel your baby's movements. This is called quickening.

Month Six

Your Baby   They start to open their eyes and react when you touch your bump.

You   Your breasts may start to produce colostrum and you will probably be able to feel your baby kicking now.

14

Natural pregnancy and birth

Month Seven

Your Baby She now has distinct waking and sleeping patterns inside your womb and can recognise familiar music.

You Braxton Hicks can start. These are practice contractions as your uterus tightens and relaxes from about week 30 onwards. As your skin stretches over your growing bump, your abdomen may feel itchy.

Month Eight

Your Baby Her bones harden, apart from the skull, which remains pliable to cope with labour. She is now fully formed.

You Your bump is now quite high and it can be difficult to eat a full meal. Opt for small frequent snacks instead.

Month Nine

Your Baby They gain up to a third of their birth weight during the last seven weeks of womb time.

You You may find yourself with a sudden desire to wash the windows or clean out the understairs cupboard. This is known as nesting.

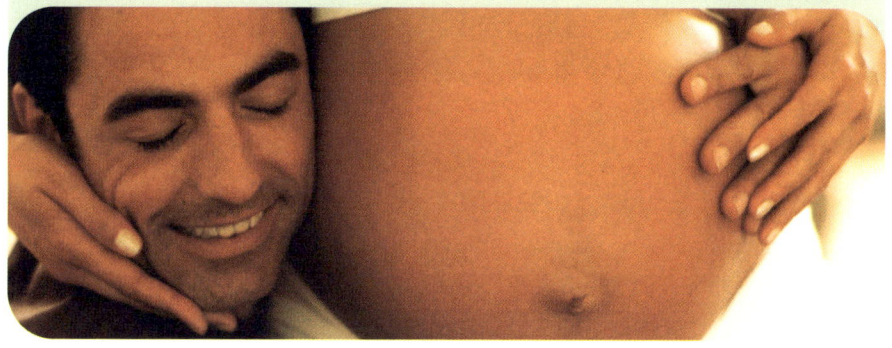

Green parenting

A checklist for pregnancy

DO

- Exercise; swimming and walking are particularly beneficial
- Yoga and Pilates can help you to prepare for birth through strengthening muscles, relaxation and visualisation
- Rest, as much as your body needs
- Go to an antenatal class or active birth class. Here you can find out about childbirth and feel supported by other women
- Eat as much fresh, 'living' food as you can
- Choose smaller regular meals, especially if you are suffering from nausea or heartburn
- Drink plenty of fluids, herbal tea and filtered water
- Eat iron rich foods, such as dried fruit and nuts and green leafy vegetables, or take an iron supplement such as Floradix. Remember that Vitamin C is vital for absorption of iron
- Get plenty of natural sunlight for vitamin D production to ensure healthy bones for you and your baby.

AVOID

- Travelling long distances, if possible, especially in late pregnancy – Airlines recommend that pregnant women don't fly after 32 weeks
- Taking long hot baths. A warm bath can be very relaxing, but make sure that the water is not too hot
- Trampolining and horse riding, as these forms of exercise can have a compression effect on the spine
- Working beyond 28 weeks if your work is strenuous
- Eating soft and blue veined cheese, pâtés and soft-boiled eggs
- Cigarettes, alcohol and drugs
- Processed foods such as ready prepared meals and food products.

Natural pregnancy and birth

Green parenting

Natural treatments during pregnancy:

In most cases, a woman's body is optimally healthy during pregnancy. There is a natural tendency for self-healing when minor illnesses or imbalances occur. Natural therapies can work with the body to enhance and strengthen this ability. If used appropriately, alternative medicines have no dangerous or unpleasant side effects and are safe for use during pregnancy. People respond differently to various therapies and you will probably find that some are more useful than others. It is wise to consult a skilled practitioner for initial guidance in using natural medicine during pregnancy. And make sure that you consult them alongside your doctor and birth support team.

Acupuncture

This therapy originated over 5,000 years ago in China and works on the basis of a vital life force or flow of energy in the body called 'chi'. The chi flows through channels that are each linked to different organs and an acupuncturist uses fine needles to release blockages and correct imbalances. Most useful in pregnancy as a treatment to stimulate labour if you are overdue, or to encourage breech babies to turn. Acupuncture can also help alleviate back pain and sickness. Consult a practitioner who has experience of working with pregnant women.

Shiatsu

Slight pressure is used to stimulate energy points and can be practised at home. A common example is the bands available from chemists, worn on your wrists, to combat travel sickness. These can also help relieve morning sickness in early pregnancy.

Aromatherapy

The use of essential oils during pregnancy can encourage relaxation, raise energy levels and restore balance. Aromatherapy oils can be used for massage, added to a warm bath or used in vaporisers. It is an effective therapy for stress-related disorders, high blood pressure, insomnia and nausea. Use a calming blend of lavender, neroli and rose during late pregnancy to help you get a good night's sleep. Geranium can also be used with jasmine as a mood enhancer. A few drops of ginger or peppermint oil on a tissue may help relieve nausea.

> **Important Note**
> **Check with a qualified aromatherpaist about which oils are safe to use during pregnancy**

Herbs

Plants have been used since time immemorial for medicinal purposes. Herbs can be used to treat a wide range of common ailments. It is advisable to seek advice from a herbalist as some plants have powerful effects and must be used with caution. Calendula tincture is a wonderful healer and a few drops can be added to a warm bath to aid healing and soothe soreness.

You can buy herbal teas from health food shops and some blends are particularly useful in pregnancy. For example, red raspberry leaf tea is good for late pregnancy. It helps to tone the uterus and has useful healing properties. Some herbalists recommend three cups a day in the last weeks of pregnancy but not before.

Chamomile tea is mild and allows for more restful sleep. It also aids digestion.

Nettle tea is a good all-rounder and can ease leg cramps and strengthen kidneys. It is a plant rich in iron so an excellent tonic for pregnant women, especially those suffering from anaemia.

Homeopathy

This is a holistic treatment; medicine for the whole person. Therefore, it is best to use medicines according to your constitutional type as recommended by a homeopath. However, Arnica and Ledum can be used to great effect during labour to reduce pain and prevent bruising. A homeopath can advise on treatment for nausea, digestive disorders, anaemia, high blood pressure, emotional difficulties and a variety of other conditions.

Green parenting

Massage

This soothing technique has been used for thousands of years to ease pains during pregnancy and assist in labour. Sweet almond oil can be used on its own, a non-scented oil that will nourish your skin, or you can choose a blend of oils that will help to relax or energise you. Gently massaging your belly will help you connect with your baby. This is a good way for your partner to communicate with your child too. A back massage can be extremely beneficial at all stages of pregnancy and you may find a lover's touch very nurturing and comforting.

Massaging your perineum (skin between your vagina and anus) is important preparation for childbirth and helps to prevent tearing during labour. After you have had a bath or shower the skin will be soft and supple. This is the best time to massage, and it's best to start about six weeks before birth. Use a base oil like almond or olive oil and massage inside your vagina and perineum, gently stretching the skin and preparing your body for birth. This exercise can help you to engage in an opening up visualisation.

Osteopathy

This is based on the belief that our skeletal and organ systems are connected and that if the structure is correctly aligned the muscles can work harmoniously and the fluids flow freely. As your posture changes during pregnancy and with the added strain on your back, osteopathy can ease unusual aches and pains. This treatment has a beneficial effect on the whole body as it improves blood flow to the organs and nerves.

Reflexology

Different areas of our feet and hands are connected to parts of our body. Therapeutic massage of the hand or foot may be used to help heal ailments such as stress, headaches and digestive problems. Evidence also suggests that regular reflexology can make labour and birth easier.

Natural pregnancy and birth

Common problems and how to treat them:

Anaemia

Red raspberry leaf tea contains iron that is easily assimilated into the system, but only use in the last trimester as as it can induce labour. An iron-rich tonic such as Floradix is also good for treating anaemia. When eating foods that contain iron such as watercress, pumpkin seeds and oats, remember that Vitamin C, found in many fruits and green vegetables, is also needed by the body to break down the iron into a usable form.

Backache

Can be caused by changes in your posture needed to accommodate the baby's weight. Stand straight and tall and wear comfortable shoes. Yoga and Pilates can help to encourage a better posture.

A good massage oil for backache during pregnancy is: two drops each of rose, geranium, lavender and roman chamomile combined with 30ml of base oil such as sweet almond oil.

Bleeding Gums

Increase your Vitamin C intake. Red raspberry leaf tea is also good for treating bleeding gums, but only in the third trimester

Constipation

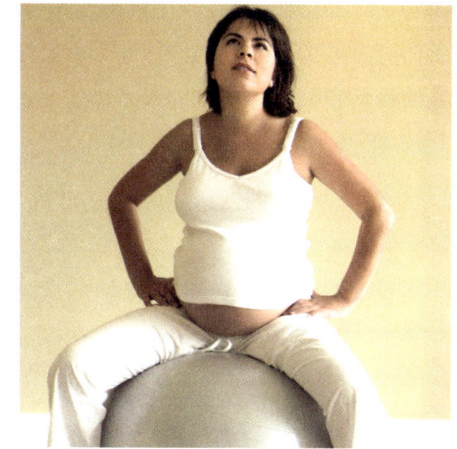

Cut back on wheat products, eat more dried fruits and take more fluids. Some prescription iron supplements can have a constipating effect. Try an iron-rich tonic such as Floradix or take red raspberry leaf tea, rich in iron. Use this only in the last three months of pregnancy.

Cramps

During pregnancy, cramps occur mainly in the thighs, calves and feet due to poor circulation or calcium deficiency. Eat plenty of garlic to improve circulation. A daily leg massage also helps prevent cramping at night.

Dizziness

Change position slowly so that your blood vessels have time to adjust and eat little and often.

Fluid Retention

The balance of salt and potassium in the cells causes hands, legs and feet to swell. Apis and Natrum Mur are the recommended homeopathic remedies, but it is best to consult a homeopath who will take a holistic view. Massage can help to reduce water retention in the legs.

Indigestion

Drink fennel tea and avoid rich, spicy or fried foods. Yoga and Pilates can alleviate the pain caused by pressure on the diaphragm.

Insomnia

Discomfort near the end of pregnancy can make sleep difficult. A teaspoon of honey and cider vinegar in warm water can help you sleep better. Also try celery juice, which is good for sleep problems.

Daily exercise, preferably outdoors, is a real tonic for sleeplessness. Wet cotton socks worn with a pair of woollen socks on top can induce sleep. Take little naps during the day and avoid watching TV before you go to bed. In fact, switch off any electrical equipment at the wall. Also, make sure your bedroom is well ventilated.

Morning Sickness

Ginger is very good for nausea. Try making a cup of ginger tea by steeping fresh ginger in hot water for ten minutes.

Try homeopathic remedies; Ipecac for continued nausea not relieved by vomiting; Sepia if the nausea is made worse by the smell or thought of food; Nux Vomica for nausea that is worse in the morning and Pulsatilla for nausea that comes on in the evening.

When you have to travel long distances during pregnancy, wear a pair of travel bands on your wrists, which work on acupressure points and are available from most good health food stores or chemists.

Boost your levels of Vitamin B6. This is found in bananas, cereals, lentils and fish.

Pelvic Pain

Massage the thighs and pelvic area quite firmly to relieve muscle pain and tightness.

Piles

Caused by a body under stress through lack of nutrients.

Apply an ice-cold witch hazel compress on gauze over the swelling.

Stretch Marks

Fine red lines that will turn silver eventually caused by the skin stretching.

Apply Aloe Vera gel direct from the succulent leaves onto your belly, breasts and thighs to prevent stretch marks.

Food containing zinc, such as sunflower and pumpkin seeds, can help to boost your skin's elasticity. Or try moisturizing your growing bump with coconut and rose oil.

Varicose Veins

A witch hazel compress will ease varicose veins. Lemon juice can also be used.

Thrush

This is due to extra pressure on the immune system during pregnancy.

Chamomile, fennel and thyme can be used to treat thrush with their antifungal properties. Apply as a compress to the vagina. Natural yoghurt can also be applied. Eat plenty of raw foods, especially garlic. You can also massage olive oil liberally around the vulva and labia. Wear cotton underwear and avoid tight fitting clothes. Cut out sugar and other sweeteners such as honey and molasses as sugar distresses the immune system.

Tiredness

Have a warm bath with a few drops of jasmine, ylang ylang or lavender. Yoga and swimming are perfect exercises for pregnancy and can energise you when you are feeling exhausted. They will also ensure a good night's sleep.

Preparing for birth

It is best to remain fairly open and flexible about how and where you will give birth as occasionally this is out of your control. However, it can be empowering to visualise a simple joyous birth to give you something to focus on during labour.

Positive thinking can have an incredibly uplifting effect on your mind and can also make birth easier. Another positive action you can take is to write a birth plan, which consolidates your feelings and aspirations for the birth itself.

The importance of pelvic floor exercises

Strengthening your pelvic floor muscles gives your body greater support during pregnancy and makes childbirth easier. After birth, strong pelvic floor muscles allow your body to return to its pre-pregnancy shape quicker. Ask your midwife for a demonstration of how to do these exercises.

Natural birth

Where to give birth?

Home birth
This is often where women (and their partners) feel most relaxed and comfortable, leading to a calmer and easier birth. A midwife can come to your home with the equipment that she needs. She might be an NHS midwife or practising independently. You will usually have to pay for the services of an independent midwife or doula (this is a woman experienced in childbirth who offers support before, during and immediately after the birth).

Birthing Centre/Midwife-led unit
These centres offer a home-from-home environment, staffed by midwives who are often skilled in alternative therapies. A birthing centre offers the opportunity for a natural birth in a calm setting with expert help on hand. Technology such as infant respirators and epidural equipment is not usually available. If an emergency procedure is necessary, transferral to a hospital will be organised.

Hospital
Some women feel safer in a hospital setting whilst others feel that the sterile, medicalised environment detracts from their natural womanly instincts. Hospitals are starting to realise that many women want to give birth naturally and more intuitively. On some labour wards you will now find birthing pools and midwives who are sensitive to a woman's desire for a natural birth.

Birth tool kit

For natural pain relief during labour

Water Birth – using a birthing pool during labour lowers blood pressure and relaxes muscles. This can slow down the actual birthing process, reducing the risk of tearing and making the baby's transition into the world a calmer one.

Active Birth – moving around during labour eases the pain of contractions and the mother feels more in control of the birth.

Massage – firm strokes especially around the lower back and pelvis. This can be combined with aromatherapy to give even greater benefits.

Hypnobirth – the use of self-hypnosis to encourage a state of deep relaxation. This technique is learnt in a class prior to childbirth.

Visualisation – you can use the power of your mind to visualise your cervix opening up like the petals of a flower or envisage your contractions as waves breaking on the shore. This can lessen the sense of pain during contractions.

Acupuncture – pressure points on the ear are activated by a trained acupuncturist to induce labour or ease the pain of contractions.

Reflexology – specific areas of the hands and feet promote relaxation and deep breathing. Applying pressure to these points during labour can ease pain.

Natural pregnancy and birth

Looking after yourself after the birth

In other cultures around the world, new mothers have a lying in period or a babymoon. This offers women and their babies the chance to get to know one another, to ease the baby's transition into this world gently and aid the recovery of mother and baby. All too often in Western culture, women are pressured into being up and about much sooner than they should be, due to busy family life or even celebrity role models. If parents can take a couple of weeks to enjoy their new baby in the comfort of their own home, all will benefit. If they can manage a month, so much the better.

Keep visitors to a minimum and if possible avoid taking your baby out to visit others. It is easy and understandable to feel uncomfortable asserting yourself like this when everyone is so eager to meet your new baby, but putting the needs of you and your child first is a vital skill and it's a good idea to learn and practise it early on. Ask your partner to help you field telephone calls and visits and perhaps well-meaning family and friends might like to pitch in and help you by bringing food or fetching shopping. After a month or so of resting and enjoying each other's company you will probably be ready to have a welcome party for your new child, and to invite friends and family. The key is to wait until you and your baby are ready.

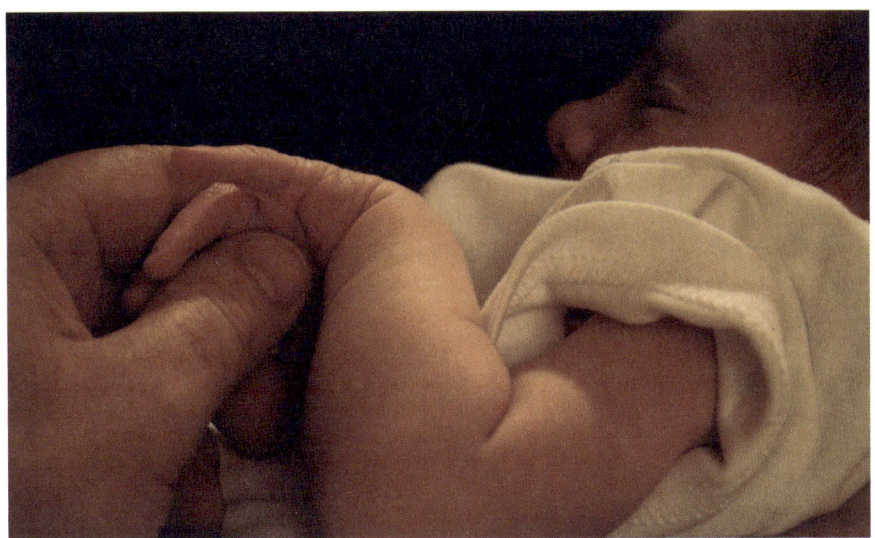

Green parenting

Physical health

Giving birth is a beautiful and huge challenge for a woman's body and of course, your body will need time to heal afterwards.

Take it easy for as long as possible. Try and avoid any housework for one month and if possible have someone to make you regular meals and snacks. If you have older children, a friend who can take them out to the park or for a walk will ease the pressure and give your children someone to talk to and confide in when they may be feeling a bit left out. Enlist as much help and support from your partner, friends and family as possible.

Continue to drink red raspberry leaf tea after birth, as this will help you heal and boost your immune system at a vulnerable time.

When bathing, run a warm bath with a few drops of calendula essential oil and a handful of salt (Himalayan if you can get hold of it).

Breastfeeding releases hormones that help your uterus back to its normal size and aids healing.

Drink as much fluid as you need and eat regularly. Snacks such as fruit, nuts, oatcakes and houmous, salads and smoothies have immune and energy boosting properties.

Look after yourself. You have just achieved an amazing feat. Now treasure the body that gave you your bundle of joy!

2

Natural babies

Green parenting

Breastfeeding

A mother's milk is the perfect food for her baby. It contains all the essential nutrients and changes throughout development to provide exactly what the child needs at each stage. The first milk is called colostrum, a thick yellow milk that has high immune boosting properties, especially important in the first days after the baby leaves the womb. The milk which usually comes in around three days after birth, contains higher levels of proteins and fats to promote growth. The mother's milk continues to change to support the growing child and when a baby starts to eat solid food, the mother's breast milk adapts to provide more antibodies to protect the child's digestive system.

In addition to the essential nutrients and immune boosting properties that breast milk offers, the act of breastfeeding is an important way to bond with a new baby. Skin to skin contact is vital for healthy development and breastfeeding encourages production of the nurturing hormone, prolactin.

Ten reasons to breastfeed:

1. Breast milk is the perfect food
It provides everything your baby needs, in the quantities it needs it, for at least the first six months of life. Many mothers exclusively feed their babies for the first year of life

2. It's the healthiest option for your baby
The health benefits of breastfeeding are huge. Your baby has a lower risk of gastro enteritis, respiratory, urinary tract and ear infections, eczema and childhood diabetes

3. It's the healthiest option for you
Breastfeeding reduces the mother's risk of breast and ovarian cancers

4. It's convenient
It's always available and instantly at the right temperature

5. It's free
In fact it saves you an estimated £450 a year

6. It saves the nation money
It's estimated that the NHS spends at least £35 million per year treating gastro-enteritis in bottle-fed babies in England

7. Breastfed babies have higher IQs
A recent study in the American Journal of Clinical Nutrition showed that breastfed infants tested 5.2 IQ points higher than bottle-fed infants

8. Breastfed babies are less likely to be obese as adults

9. It's more environmentally friendly
Breast milk is produced and delivered to the consumer without any pollution, unnecessary packaging or waste! Or milk miles!

10. Women who breastfeed regain their figures sooner
That's because when your body is making breast milk it burns about 500 calories a day.

Why choose baby-led feeding?

Breasts are not bottles, they do not respond well when restricted to a regime of four-hourly feeds with 10 minutes allocated to each breast. Milk soon dries up under these conditions because production is not being sufficiently stimulated. A breastfeeding 'regime' like this could also lead to painful engorgement.

Your baby will go through several growth spurts in the early months. It is best to take the lead from them as to when they want to feed and for how long, as they may need extra milk during these periods of growth. Some parenting 'gurus' believe that baby-led feeding will create a spoilt child. You can't spoil a baby. They will be more secure and content if their needs are being met. Do what feels best for you, follow your intuition and listen to your baby.

How much and how often?

The average baby feeds between eight and twelve times a day during the first two weeks. This decreases to between six and nine feeds during the second month. This is around 112 to 212 minutes every 24 hours during the first two weeks. It will probably feel like much longer during the early days of breastfeeding. Use this time to rest, put your feet up, enjoy your new baby, eat frequently and drink lots.

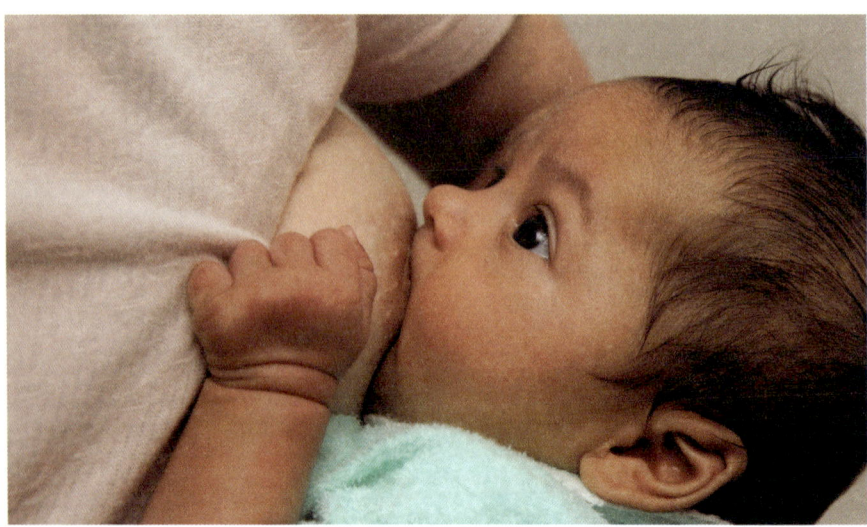

Common problems and how to treat them:

Milk production
The more a baby feeds the more milk is produced, so an easy way to increase production is to feed your baby more frequently to get supply established. Fennel tea can also be taken to boost milk production.

Sore, cracked nipples
A little expressed breast milk massaged into the affected area can help to heal cracked nipples. Calendula cream can also soothe sore skin and promotes healing. It is safe for babies to swallow. This can be very painful, but try to keep milk flowing to prevent engorgement. If it is too uncomfortable to breastfeed on the affected breast, gently express milk by hand.

Problems with let-down
Breastfeeding is most effective when mother and baby are relaxed. If you are having problems relaxing, try having a warm bath with a few drops of lavender essential oil. You can feed your baby in the bath and you may find that the warm water helps them relax too. A massage can help or a cup of soothing tea.

Engorgement
During the first weeks after birth your breasts can become full and hard. Feeding frequently should bring relief. You can use warm compresses to help the milk flow. Leaves from a cabbage kept in the fridge can be applied to the breasts to reduce swelling and absorb heat.

Inflammation
Savoy cabbage leaves can be tucked inside your bra to calm inflammation. Calendula and chamomile essential oils are anti-inflammatory and can be diluted in a carrier oil, such as sweet almond, and massaged into your breasts. But avoid the nipple and aureole. Echinacea tincture taken in a glass of water will help the body to fight infection.

Tiredness

Rest when your baby is resting. Once breastfeeding is established you might find it comfortable to lie down on your side and doze whilst your baby is feeding during the daytime. At night, sleep with your baby. Some studies have found that mothers who breastfeed and co-sleep get the most restful sleep.

Ensure you are eating plenty of energy rich foods and drinking lots of fluids to keep your energy levels up. Try slow-releasing energy foods such as oats, nuts, seeds, sprouts and bananas.

Holistic bottle-feeding

Some mothers cannot or choose not to breastfeed their baby. If it is necessary for you to bottle-feed your baby, there are ways to make this as holistic an experience as possible.

- **Indulge in skin-to-skin contact.** When feeding your baby, take your top off and cradle them to you so that they can smell and feel your skin

- **Choose glass bottles rather than plastic.** Glass bottles are becoming increasingly available from natural baby shops and websites. They do not leach chemicals in the way that some plastic containers can do

- **Research alternatives.** If you think your baby might be allergic to the cow's milk protein in his or her formula milk, look for alternatives. There is a goat's milk formula available. Allergies such as eczema and asthma can be a sign that you baby's system is under stress

- **Find other ways to get your prolactin (the nurturing hormone) flowing.** This aids successful bonding. Baby massage, co-sleeping, using a baby carrier, singing to your baby; these are all ways that you and your baby can enjoy the close presence of one another

- **Encourage your partner to activate his prolactin levels.** Massage and baby wearing are good ways for dads to encourage prolactin to start flowing

- **Keep your energy levels up.** All new mums need to eat and drink frequently. You may find eating snacks or small meals about five times a day more useful in the early days to keep your energy levels up. Choose wholefoods, organic and raw where possible

- **Let guilt go.** If you feel guilty about being unable to breastfeed, learn to let that go. Talk to your partner, friends, other mothers, your doctor and explain how you feel. Holding onto negative emotions is not healthy for you or your child. Celebrate yourself as a mother and remember all the nurturing things that you do every day for your child.

Green parenting

When to wean?

The World Health Organisation now recommends exclusive breastfeeding for babies up to the age of six months. This confers optimum immunity to the small child. In many cultures, the breastfeeding relationship continues into the third year and beyond and extended breastfeeding is now becoming more popular in Western countries. Breastfeeding past your child's second birthday provides a magical way to bond with an increasingly independent toddler and continues to boost your child's immune system and promote health for the years to come.

Your baby will probably communicate their readiness for solid foods by showing a greater interest in what you are eating, maybe even taking food from your plate and sucking it. First foods usually consist of vegetable purees. If you have the time it is better to puree organically grown produce at home than rely on packet food.

Some ideas for first weaning food:

SWEET DELIGHTS
Sweet potato and carrot puree
1 sweet potato, chopped finely
1 carrot, chopped finely

GREEN SUPER FOOD
Broccoli and pea puree
1 head of broccoli (around 100g), finely chopped
100g fresh (or frozen) peas

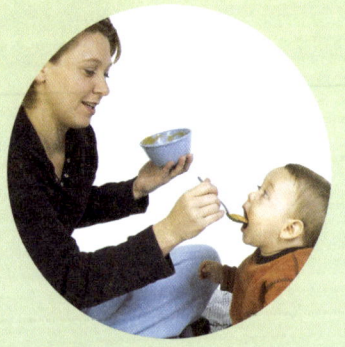

THE STAIRS TO HEAVEN
Apple and pear puree
1 apple, peeled, cored and finely chopped
1 small ripe pear, finely chopped

Place the vegetables/fruit in a saucepan, cover with water and bring to the boil. Cook until soft. Push through a fine sieve.

Separate 2 tablespoons into a bowl. Your baby will probably only eat a few teaspoons to start. The rest can be put in the freezer in ice cube trays and defrosted when needed.

Baby massage

Touch is vital to all humans. We all feel so much better for a hug or a massage. and babies benefit even more from physical touch. Baby massage is very simple and has many benefits:

- Soothes and relaxes you and your baby

- Increases milk production by stimulating the hormone, prolactin. Men can also produce prolactin, so baby massage can help a father to bond with his baby

- Improves sleeping patterns

- Boosts immune system function

- Helps to treat cases of wind and colic.

You do not need any special equipment to massage your baby. A warm room, some natural massage oil and a towel are all that's required. Organic sweet almond oil is ideal for babies' delicate skin. A simple routine can be gently stroking your baby from head to toe. There are also classes where mums and dads can learn this gentle art of soothing their baby. To find one in your area contact the IAIM (International Association of Infant Massage), www.iaim.org.uk or your health visitor for free classes.

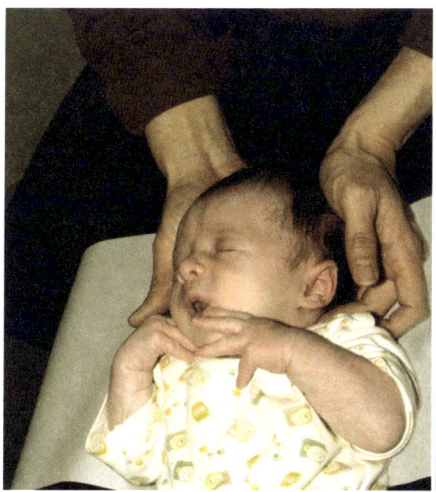

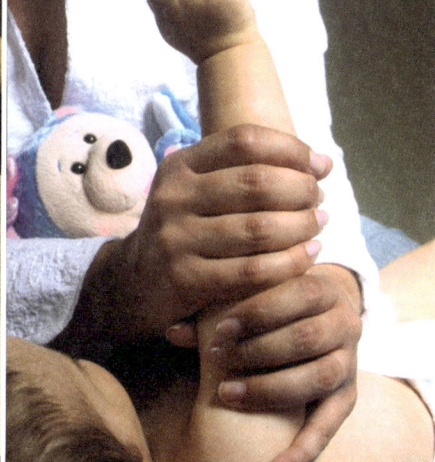

Green parenting

Baby wearing

In traditional cultures, parents carry their babies in a sling, blanket or cloth sarong so that the baby has continuous body contact. This allows you to continue your normal daily activities, whilst providing the optimum environment for your baby. Practising this natural parenting approach to baby care will encourage secure, confident children. They will grow up understanding that their needs will be met and that they do not need to cry to get attention.

Benefits to baby wearing:

- Creates an intimate bond between parent and child
- Held in a position where they can hear their mother's heartbeat, a baby feels secure and content
- Encourages babies to develop good posture and muscle tone
- It is good for a baby's digestive system and helps to prevent colic and wind
- Easier to feed. Some slings allow for breastfeeding on the move, if you can manage it!
- A wide range of different slings ensures you need not suffer from back pain. As your baby gets heavier you can find the best model for carrying your growing child
- Increasingly used as an aid to elimination timing (raising a baby without nappies).

Real nappies:

Why choose real nappies?

Health

Cloth nappies are the healthiest option for your baby. Some of the chemicals contained in disposables are not monitored by any guidelines in the UK and leading nappy brands are reluctant to divulge the exact contents of their products. If your baby is suffering from nappy rash, the broken skin is more likely to absorb these nasties.

Environment

No nappy is completely environmentally-friendly, but washable nappies come out on top. The waste issues surrounding disposables are undisputable. Every disposable nappy that has ever been made still exists today. Around 4 percent of the UK's household waste is made up of nappies which cost local councils around £200,000 a year to dispose of. In fact, one baby's disposable nappies would cover two thirds of a football pitch within one year.

The waste problem at the end of their short life is obviously the main environmental pitfall of the disposable nappy. But prior to this, they use more energy to produce than re-usable nappies and up to 8 times as many non-regenerable raw materials. To grow a disposable nappy requires around 4 to 30 times as much land as a washable nappy and that isn't even taking into account the amount of landfill space needed to accommodate them after use.

Cost

Using re-usable nappies can work out a good deal cheaper than cladding your baby's bottom in plastic and paper pulp. You could save between £600 and £1000 by using cloth, especially if you plan to use them for several children.

Given the evidence against disposables, if we want to leave a legacy to our children, using washable nappies is just one positive choice we can make for our babies and for our planet.

Green parenting

I would like to try washable nappies but am put off by the huge upfront cost

Don't be! There are other ways of sampling real nappies. Some companies offer a low cost trial scheme. You can also buy second-hand nappies, which significantly reduces the cost. Enquire about nappy schemes at your local council because in recent years, many have woken up to the waste issue in a big way. Some offer vouchers redeemable against the purchase of real nappies or have funded projects to make washable nappies more accessible to lower income families.

I am a working mum and don't have time to use real nappies

It may seem extravagant to hire someone to do your washing for you, but using a nappy laundry service still works out cheaper than disposable nappies and is the greenest option. You can put dirty nappies into a bin with a lid and these will be collected once a week and be brought back freshly laundered and ready to wear. Very simple and time and money saving.

It all seems a bit complicated to me

It needn't be. There are real nappy experts who will be happy to advise you on which nappy to use for your baby and how to go about it. They will come to your home with a selection of different styles and explain the benefits of each to help you decide. You could invite a real nappy person to come and speak to all the parents at your parent and baby group. See directory for more information.

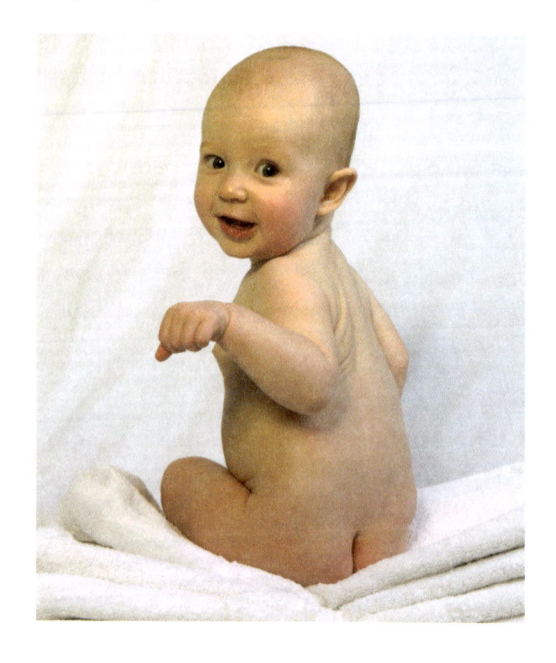

Tips on dealing with nappy rash:

- Allow your child to spend as much time as possible with a bare bottom.

- Change your baby's nappy as soon as it gets wet or dirty.

- Avoid using baby wipes with 'fragrance' as these may contain chemicals that aggravate your baby's skin. Use a cotton flannel soaked in warm water to clean your baby's bottom.

- Calendula ointment applied to the rash is soothing and aids healing. Breast milk also has healing properties and you can express a little onto the affected area to soothe the skin.

- Avoid certain foods in your baby's diet (or yours if you are breast-feeding) such as highly acidic foods, fruit juices etc.

Other eco-friendly alternatives

Biodegradable disposables

Brands such as Tushies, Moltex and Mother Nature offer an occasional alternative to washable nappies and can be useful for camping trips or when travelling. These products do not contain chemicals and most are 100 percent biodegradable within around eight weeks if handled correctly. These nappies can be safely recycled using a method called vermicomposting, a process in which worms break down the whole nappy and its contents to produce rich compost. This compost is safe to use on your vegetable plot, as the worms produce worm casts which are then digested by microbes breaking down and eliminating any pathogens or germs.

Green parenting

Elimination timing

The most environmentally-friendly method of dealing with your baby's waste is elimination timing. This involves getting in tune with your baby's cycle so that you know when he or she needs to pee. Held in a supportive way over the toilet or potty on a regular basis, your baby soon learns to associate certain noises and positions with going to the toilet. This method has been used in ancient cultures since time began, but a growing number of parents in Western society are starting to discover its benefits. It creates no waste, costs nothing and encourages a strong intuitive bond to form between parent and child.

3

Green nutrition

Green parenting

Eating well as a family

Food is at the centre of all our lives whether we recognise it or not. It is what sustains us and keeps us alive and so, good food is key to a healthy lifestyle. What we put into our bodies is hugely important and teaching children about diet and nutrition when they are young will hopefully encourage them to be healthy in the future.

Mealtimes should not become a battleground. It is important that eating is seen as a pleasurable activity and one that the family shares whenever they can. Family mealtimes, although not always possible, are an easy way to enjoy time together and catch up on each other's news. It is also important, not only to eat with children wherever possible, but for children to be involved in the cooking process. Encourage your children to help in the food preparation, whether that be grating carrots to put in the salad or making a pasta sauce. In just a few easy steps, food and mealtimes can become an enjoyable and celebrated part of everyday life which fits neatly into the often busy family routine.

Green food

What are food miles?

Food miles describe the distance our food has to travel to reach our plate. Transport by road and air uses up huge quantities of fuel and causes tonnes of harmful carbon dioxide emissions. Food production and distribution produces eight tonnes of Co^2 emissions per household every year.

It is estimated that the ingredients for a typical Sunday lunch could have travelled 24,000 miles to get to our homes.

Green Nutrition

Why does our food travel so far?

As supermarkets have taken over from local retailers, produce often travels many miles to a centralised distribution point and is then dispatched again, sometimes to a store just a few miles from where the food was originally sourced. Ninety five percent of fruit and half the vegetables we consume in the UK are imported. This all adds up to thousands of air miles to get bananas on our supermarket shelves. We can now buy strawberries in January, asparagus in December, and oranges in March, all flown in from warmer climes. Because food has to travel such long distances and must reach the shelves in good condition, fruit and vegetables are often harvested unripe, transported in cold storage and delivered to the supermarket days, even weeks old, and yet still unripe. It may seem obvious when you think about it, but produce tastes best when picked fresh and ripe.

What can I do?

- **Buy local** – check out farmers markets, greengrocers or local organic box delivery schemes
- **Grow your own** – the most environmentally-friendly way to eat
- **Buy seasonal** – don't buy food that is out of season in the UK. Chances are that it has been transported from the other side of the world, and preserved in cold storage for its long carbon-emitting journey

What are additives?

For children, exposure to food additives like preservatives, artificial colouring and flavourings and artificial sweeteners can cause dramatic behavioural changes, skin problems and allergies such as eczema and asthma. Some of these substances have been found to cause cancer in laboratory animals. A survey by the Food Commission found that of the 350 children's foods tested, 61 percent have flavours and flavour enhancers added, 38 percent have colouring added. One in five products has five or more colours added to make them more appealing to their young audience. This survey looked at the food our children eat every day, cereal, fruit and vegetables, dairy products, canned and frozen foods and desserts. It did not even include so-called junk food such as confectionery, soft drinks or juices, bag snacks, crisps or birthday cakes.

Green parenting

What to avoid

The Foods Standards Agency has just embarked on a study to determine whether there is a link between additives in food and children's behaviour. The report will be published late 2007. In the meantime, you might like to consider the opinion of thousands of parents the world over who have watched the effects of additives first hand and have decided to eliminate them from their family's diet. A number of studies and reports have highlighted the adverse effects of the consumption of additives and parents have become suspicious. For example, flavourings and colourings are used to disguise cheap ingredients such as starch, malodextrine and added water which have little or no nutritional value. Many of these have been linked to health problems in children; artificial colourings to hyperactivity, mood swings, sleeplessness and poor concentration; artificial sweeteners and monosodium glutamate to headaches, dizziness and seizures.

Although it is better to avoid all artificial additives in your child's diet these are the ones that you really want to steer clear of:

Flavour enhancers
L-Glutamic Acid E620
Monosodium Glutamate E621
Disodium Guanylate E627
Disodium Inosinate E631

Artificial sweeteners
Sodium Benzoate E211
Sulphur Dioxide E220
Aspartame E951
Acesulfame K
Tartrazine
Homogenised Fat

Colourings
(Most of these colourings are banned in Australia, USA and some European countries, NOT the UK)
Quinoline Yellow E104
Sunset Yellow E110
Carmoisine (red) E122
Allura Red E129
Indigo Carmine E132
Brilliant Blue E133
Brilliant Black E151
Aluminium E173

What are the alternatives?

- Choose organic foods – you can avoid E numbers and other chemical nasties

- Become label savvy - always read the label. Few of us have time to scrutinise every label whilst dashing round the supermarket, especially when accompanied by a gaggle of hungry kids, but if we become label savvy then a quick glance can tell us whether a food is suitable for our kids or not. The label lists the ingredients in order of weight. So, if fat and sugar are at the top of the list, then it contains high levels of fat and sugar and is best avoided. The claim 'Reduced in Fat' can be used on foods that contain 25% less than a comparative product. So, it doesn't necessarily mean low in fat. 'Low Fat' is used on those products that contain less than 3 percent fat, but this is only a government recommendation, so do check the label. And just because these foods are made up of less than 3 percent fat doesn't mean that they are healthy. Often low fat foods, such as diet drinks, contain artificial sweeteners and should be avoided, especially by young children. Additives can be listed by name or E number, so check for both. Genetically modified substances must be identified on the label. Be especially aware of products like bread, packets of cereal, children's flavoured yoghurts and canned food

- Cook your own – homemade food tastes better and is wholesome

- Avoid taking your children shopping in shops where sweets and junk foods are displayed at the checkouts

- Talk to your child's school/nursery about additives in food and encourage teachers to find out how they affect children's learning and behaviour

- Talk to your children about how companies boast about their products. Explain about food advertising and branding and encourage your children to make healthy choices when choosing for themselves

Green parenting

What are Genetically Modified foods?

Genetic Modification is the alteration of a food to make it more resilient and less prone to disease or attack by insects. Scientists can identify individual genes and their functions and use this knowledge to transplant genes from one plant or animal to another. At the moment, over 3,000 genetically engineered foods are being tested. The ones we hear most about are tomatoes, soya, and maize (corn). As no research has been done on the effects of this food alteration, we are effectively guinea pigs in a laboratory where our food and health have been turned into the experiment.

What can I do?

- Choose organic. Genetically modified ingredients are not permitted in organic food

- Write to your supermarket and tell them that you do not want to eat GM foods. Some meat and dairy products are produced from animals fed on GM feeds. Many supermarkets have taken a strong stance on this, but it is important that they are aware of their consumers' opinions and that they work to keep GM foods and foods derived from GM sources off the shelves

What is organic food?

Organic means grown without the use of pesticides and other chemicals. In conventional agriculture, a huge array of pesticides are used, many of which are toxic to humans and are increasingly being implicated in the development of diseases such as cancer. Despite the fact that there are Government regulations to control the use of these chemicals, foods are often found with much higher residues than are considered acceptable.

Why choose organic?

There are 20 chemicals found on the average non-organic apple, even after washing. We do not have enough evidence to suggest that it is safe for babies to ingest the cocktail of chemicals that they are subjected to when eating food that has not been grown organically. The benefit to the environment of organic farming has been demonstrated in many surveys. The pesticides used in conventional farming kill many soil organisms, insects and larger creatures. They also kill plants considered to be weeds, reducing food sources for animals, birds and insects and destroying habitats.

Organic farming, in contrast, encourages a wider range of habitats, herb and clover rich grassland and a mixed range of crops. Animals on organic farms are free to express natural behaviour, have access to fields and are fed on organic feed or grassland. They have no need for the routine antibiotics and other drugs given to non-organic livestock. There are no health or pollution problems caused by organic farming as no artificial chemicals are used. This, in turn, means less dependence on non-renewable energy sources, such as fossil fuels, which are used in the production of fertilisers and agrochemicals.

Recent research said that intensively farmed food now has less of the nutrients and minerals that it used to have. They suspect this is because the soil is less healthy following the use of artificial fertilisers.

Green parenting

Ten reasons to go organic for the health of your family:

1 You can trust the food. Certified organic food is grown to strict national standards which are routinely checked

2 You are avoiding or significantly reducing your family's exposure to harmful pesticides and other man-made chemical residues. Organic food is grown without the artificial chemicals such as fertilizers, pesticides, fungicides, drugs and antibiotics that are used in intensive farming. In 2001 alone, 26 million kilogrammes of pesticides were sold in the UK and most of this was sprayed onto Britain's fields. Infants are more at risk from residues due to their high food intake compared to their body size and their fragile, undeveloped organs and body systems. There is increasing scientific evidence that many diseases in later life stem from exposure to toxic chemicals and poor quality of food in childhood

3 You will enjoy food more as organic food tastes fresher and more flavourful

4 You are supporting sustainable farming which recycles natural resources rather than depleting them. Unlike intensive farming, which strips the soil of nutrients and applies artificial ones, organic production builds the health and fertility of the soil

5 You are reducing the pollution caused by intensive farming which contaminates ground water, rivers, streams and lakes with the over-use of nitrates, pesticides and drugs used to treat farmed fish

Green Nutrition

6 You and your family are helping to protect and encourage wildlife such as insects, birds and bats and the wildflowers and trees that they depend on. These habitats have been progressively destroyed and polluted and several UK species are already extinct or have been endangered as a result

7 You are contributing to your children's ongoing good health by building a strong immune system which will help to protect them against serious illness. The food that you eat will have more vitamins and minerals compared with non-organic foods. Chemically treated food is forced to grow faster and bigger and nutrients are often lost in the process

8 You are helping to protect the ozone layer and save energy. Chemicals that are sprayed on crops damage the ozone layer, contribute to global warming and require large amounts of non-renewable energy to produce

9 You experience the organic feel-good factor. Shopping trips are guilt-free, especially if you walk to your local shops or organise a delivery, which means one journey replaces lots of individual trips

10 Food is fun. Organic food is best eaten fresh so it means getting into the kitchen, preferably with your children to prepare family meals that can be enjoyed together.

Green parenting

The cost of organic food

Although the cost of organic food might seem prohibitive to the average family, it is worthwhile to look at all the options before you decide it's not for you. Firstly, if you consider the health benefits to your family of eating more organic food, you might decide to make cutbacks in other areas to free up more money to spend on food shopping. You might find that by avoiding expensive ready meals, drinks and brand cereals, you can afford to spend more on fresh organic produce. You might be able to pick up some good deals at your local farmers market, buying direct from the producer and cutting out the supermarket middleman.

Preparing goodies at home for lunch boxes, instead of buying snacks every day, could save the average family £10 a day.

Some lunch box ideas include:
- A flask of homemade tomato soup and a crusty roll
- A pot of homemade houmous with vegetable sticks, pitta bread and corn chips
- Homemade sweet corn muffins with an apple or banana
- Pitta bread stuffed with falafels and a selection of vegetables such as cucumber, tomatoes, carrot and bean sprouts.

If the indirect costs of conventional farming were included in food prices (clean up of polluted water, rubbish collection and processing, landfill site maintenance, environmental protection activities, healthcare costs) organic food would probably work out a lot cheaper than conventional foods. It is also getting cheaper to buy organic food because the number of us buying it is increasing.

What can I do?
- Shop around. Ask for good deals at farmers markets.
- Form a collective. Get together with friends and buy organic food from wholesalers. Grains, cereals, pasta, sauces, oils, canned foods etc. can all be bought cheaper in bulk through a wholesaler like Infinity Foods or Suma. The order is delivered to one address and all the members come together to collect their food.
- When you have the time, prepare food at home rather than resorting to ready made foods; it's cheaper and fresher.

The organic revolution in schools

Thanks in part to Jamie Oliver and the sterling work of the Soil Association, school dinners came under scrutiny last year when they were found to be high in fats, salt and sugar. Since then, the UK Government has done much to ensure that all children get the nutrients that they need in their lunchtime meal. As well as school catering firms being urged to use local, seasonal and organic produce for pupils' lunches, more emphasis is to be put on cooking lessons within the National Curriculum. This is an important step towards teaching our children about healthy eating and empowering them by showing them how to cook nutritious meals for themselves.

What about a vegetarian or vegan diet?

Being a vegetarian means a diet containing no animal products, such as meat, poultry and fish. A vegan diet excludes all animal products and bi-products such as dairy, eggs and honey. Vegans also avoid leather products. Some concerns have been raised about a vegetarian or vegan diet for young children. But counter reports have proven that children can grow and thrive on a nutritious diet containing no animal products. In fact, this diet has been found to be healthier than that of meat-eaters. Meat and dairy foods contain artery clogging saturated fat and cholesterol, the main markers for heart disease and other heart problems. Up to 75 babies in every 1000 are allergic to cow's milk. Often the first sign of a problem is excessive mucus, resulting in a constant running nose, blocked ears or a persistent sore throat.

A vegetarian diet easily provides all the nutrients that a child needs – protein, carbohydrates, vitamins and minerals. Not only is it a safe choice, it is a healthier choice because it is lower in harmful saturated fat, cholesterol and animal protein. Scientists have discovered that a properly planned vegetarian diet actually protects children, reducing the risk of many killer diseases in later life, including obesity, coronary artery and heart disease, high blood pressure, strokes, diabetes and some types of cancer.

Green parenting

Nutrition for the family

Super foods:

Some foods provide super nutrients and have extra immune boosting properties. This list is by no means exhaustive and indeed there are many other foods that offer optimum nutrition, but these super foods will boost the health of your family, especially if each is included at least once a week.

Food	Contains	Good for
Apple	Carotenes Pectin Vitamin C Potassium	Immune system Digestive system Heart and circulation
Almonds	B vitamins Vitamin E Calcium Magnesium	Bone building Immune boosting Energy
Beetroot	Vitamins B6 and C Beta-carotene, Iron Potassium, Folic acid Calcium	Anaemia Chronic fatigue Convalescence
Broccoli	Vitamins A & C Folic acid, riboflavin Potassium, Iron, Phytochemicals	Anaemia Chronic fatigue Protection against cancer
Carrots	Vitamin A Carotenoids Folic acid Potassium Magnesium	Eyesight Circulation, Heart Protection against cancer Good for skin

Food	Contains	Good for
Garlic and onions	Antibacterial and antifungal properties Cancer fighting and heart protective Phytochemicals	Relieving sinus and chest problems Preventing heart disease and high blood pressure
Grapes	Vitamin C Antioxidant flavanoids	Convalescence Anaemia Fatigue Cancer protection Weight gain
Lemons	Vitamin C Bioflavanoids Potassium	Powerful immune booster Digestive problems Oral health, especially gum problems
Mushrooms	Some Proteins Vitamins B12 and E Zinc	Relieving depression, anxiety and fatigue
Oats	Calcium Potassium Magnesium, B vitamins	Protective against heart disease Aids digestion Skin conditions
Seeds	Protein Minerals such as Zinc and Selenium Essential fats	Cancer fighting Constipation Energy Fibre and energy
Sprouted seeds	B vitamins Folic acid	Nutrients and energy Protection against cancer

Recipes

Easy, quick snacks and meals that can be enjoyed by young and old alike. It can be a challenge to serve nutritious food in a tight family schedule, but these recipes offer some ideas for fast food with health benefits.

Vegetable crisps
Preparation: 10 minutes
Cooking: 30 minutes

500g root vegetables such as carrots, parsnips and beetroot
Olive oil
Sea salt

- Preheat oven to Gas Mark 6, 200°C. Slice vegetables thinly and place in a large mixing bowl. Add olive oil and toss to coat
- Tip out onto a lightly greased baking tray and bake in the oven for 30 minutes until crispy and brown at the edges
- Sprinkle with sea salt and serve with garlic mayonnaise or hummus.

Toasted seeds
Preparation: 1 minute
Cooking: 5 minutes

100g pumpkin seeds
100g sunflower seeds
2 tbsp tamari

- Preheat oven to Gas Mark 4, 180°C
- Spread seeds evenly over a baking tray. Pop in the oven for 5 minutes Remove and sprinkle liberally with tamari
- Scoop into a bowl and serve as a snack (alternative to crisps) or sprinkled on soups or salads.

Green Nutrition

Houmous
Preparation: 5 minutes

400g can of chickpeas or dried chickpeas soaked overnight
2 tbsp tahini
3 tbsp lemon juice
1 large garlic clove crushed
1/4 tsp ground cumin
Salt and pepper

- Drain chickpeas and save liquid for later
- Put the chickpeas in a blender and add the tahini, lemon juice, garlic, cumin and 4 tbsp of chickpea liquid. Blend until smooth
- Season with salt and pepper. Serve on toast, jacket potatoes or as a dip with colourful vegetables such as peppers, carrots and cucumber and some warm pitta bread.

Green parenting

Potato and leek soup
Preparation: 5 minutes
Cooking: 25 minutes

3 leeks sliced and chopped
1 large potato, scrubbed and cut into 2 cm cubes
1 tbsp olive oil
30g margarine
1 pint hot vegetable stock
Salt and pepper
1/2 pt soya milk

- Cook leeks and potato in olive oil for 5 minutes, stirring occasionally
- Add margarine and allow to melt before adding stock and seasoning
- Bring to the boil and simmer gently for 15 minutes until the potato is well cooked
- Turn off the heat and place half the soup in a food processor until smooth
- Allow to cool slightly and add the soya milk. Pour back into the saucepan
- Garnish with fresh herbs and serve with hunks of granary bread.

Green Nutrition

Tabbouleh

Preparation time: 5 minutes
Resting time: 30 minutes

225g bulgur wheat
1/2 litre of hot vegetable stock
4 spring onions, chopped
50g dried apricots, chopped
50g raisins
Juice of 1 lemon
4 tbsp olive oil
Salt and pepper

- Cover the bulgur wheat with the stock and leave to stand for 30 minutes until all the water has been absorbed
- Stir in the rest of the ingredients and season to taste
- Serve with pitta breads cut in half. Each half can be stuffed with tabbouleh.

Green parenting

Quick tomato sauce for pasta

Preparation: 5 minutes
Cooking: 15 minutes

1 onion, finely chopped
Olive oil
1 tbsp tomato puree
1 tsp dried basil, oregano or mixed herbs
1 can chopped tomatoes

- Sauté the onion in a little olive oil until soft
- Add tomato puree and herbs and stir to mix
- Add the chopped tomatoes and cook for 5 minutes
- Serve with pasta, grated cheese and olives for a quick family dinner.

Green Nutrition

Flapjacks

Preparation: 5 minutes
Cooking: 40 minutes

175g butter
175g unrefined Demerara sugar
2 tbsp golden syrup
225g rolled oats
1 tsp ground ginger
Handful of chopped dried fruits such as apricots, dates and raisins
Handful of seeds such as sunflower, sesame and pumpkin

- Preheat oven to Gas Mark 5, 190°C
- Melt butter with sugar and syrup in a heavy based pan
- Remove from heat and add to a mixing bowl with oats, ginger, fruit and seeds
- Spread mixture in tin, press down evenly with the back of a spoon. Bake for 25/30 minutes until golden brown
- Mark into squares whilst still hot then leave in tin until cool.

When cool, remove from the tin and store in an airtight container.

Green parenting

Grow your own

Getting started

So you want to grow your own family food, but don't know where to begin? When working with children the best place to start is with windowsill herbs which are easy to grow, offer quick results and can be used to enhance the flavour of many meals. Try a pot of parsley, basil and mint. Encourage your children to grow them from seed and they become so much more tempting to eat.

Sprouted seeds are also easy to grow and produce very quick results (most sprout within three days). Invest in a sprouting jar and a packet of mung beans from your local health food store and get sprouting for optimum family health.

In your garden, you might like to start with courgettes and beans, as they are easy to grow and the results taste far superior to those bought shrink-wrapped in plastic from a supermarket. Strawberries and tomatoes are attractive and colourful fruits that can easily be grown in the garden or even in a pot on a balcony.

Growing food for your family may not necessarily cost less than purchasing food from the supermarket, but if you consider the feel-good factor and the knowledge that the food on your plate is fresh and free from harmful chemicals, it becomes a very attractive option. For children, the pleasure and educational benefit of watching seeds that they planted growing into food that they can share with their family is a valuable lesson. It provides a chance for the family to enjoy an outdoor activity together and get fit into the bargain.

If you don't have the outdoor space at home, consider taking on an allotment. They are relatively cheap to rent, often have a great community atmosphere and offer the chance to get tips from and share tools with other gardeners.

Green Nutrition

Feeding the soil

Making your own compost is not only highly beneficial for your plants; it also makes good use of kitchen scraps that might otherwise end up in the bin. There is a wide range of purpose built containers or you can build your own, using a stack of car tyres or wooden pallets nailed together. A wormery uses worms to accelerate the composting process and can be useful for smaller gardens where you do not have the room for a large heap.

For books that will help you get started in growing your own organic food, check out www.impactpublishing.co.uk. Their *Green Essentials* books are great value and cover most aspects of organic gardening.

Green parenting

4
Holistic health

Green parenting

> Using natural medicine is a gentle, rewarding approach to your family's health. Supporting and nurturing a child through an illness, whether it is a cold or chicken pox can have a beneficial physiological effect on parent and child. Rather than resorting to pain-blocking over-the-counter drugs, treating the illness naturally aids the immune system in allowing the body to fight the infection, and makes room for the developmental leap that often takes place after a period of convalescing.

In addition, holistic medicine treats the whole person rather than just the symptoms as in allopathic medicine. For example, a child with a cough and a sore throat is likely to be prescribed a cough suppressant and antibiotics by their doctor, in order to treat their symptoms. A homeopath treating the same child will consult with the parent and, if appropriate, the child, in an effort to discover the child's general state of health and characteristics before providing a remedy that best treats the whole child; his mind, body and soul. Other holistic therapies work in the same way, treating the person and not just the symptoms he or she is exhibiting. Another common childhood disease, eczema, is treated with steroid cream in allopathic medicine, whereas you will find that the underlying cause is addressed in complementary medicine.

In today's fast paced society, we don't have time to get ill. We can pop a painkiller and get on with our daily lives, but a bout of illness is the body's way of alerting us that all is not in harmony. Illness is a message that we need to take some time out. This should also be the case for our children. If they fall ill, if at all possible, try to rearrange your schedule so that you can care for them and let the illness take its natural course.

Having said all that, this chapter's purpose is not to suggest that all conventional medicine is detrimental or that parents should not consult a doctor. Ideally, as parents, we should be able to find a balance of allopathic and alternative medicine which best cater to the needs of our family. Sadly, alternative therapies are not always promoted by our local GPs!

Holistic health

What is in the alternative medicine chest?

- **Arnica Cream** – for treating bumps and bruises – this homeopathic cream has proved itself as a superb healer and is also good for reducing swelling. The homeopathic remedy Arnica is also useful to have, for bruises and shock.

- **Rescue Remedy** – several drops on the tongue can relieve shock and distress. It has been used effectively on animals as well as humans.

- **Chamomile Tea** – A teabag steeped in boiling water for five minutes makes an excellent eyewash for conjunctivitis. The tea is also useful for soothing tired and fractious patients, young and old alike.

- **Aloe Vera** – grow one of these juicy succulent plants on your windowsill and discover their amazing skin healing properties. In case of minor burns, squeeze the juice onto the affected area.

- **Honey** – if you don't have access to aloe vera, raw honey applied to minor burns is soothing and an excellent healer. It has other therapeutic uses too, for example, honey and lemon tea is a soothing treatment for relief of coughs and sore throats.

- **Lavender oil** – a few drops of essential oil in the bath before bed or on a hankie beside the pillow can encourage a good night's sleep. Also good for treating skin problems, such as nappy rash (a few drops added to an unscented cream or balm and applied to the affected area) or spots.

- **Tea Tree oil** – a powerful antiseptic. Can be used to treat cuts and sores and to deter head lice.

- **Oats** – put a handful of oats in a muslin bag, or sock, and place under the running water in the bath. You have created a soothing treatment for many skin conditions including eczema.

Holistic Therapies

Acupuncture

An ancient Eastern treatment that uses needles to rebalance the body's chi or life force. It is effective in the treatment of a number of common ailments.

Aromatherapy

The use of essential oils to treat the mind and body, either as a massage blend through touch or through inhalation. An aromatherapy massage can be very relaxing and calming, or stimulating and invigorating. A trained aromatherapist will usually give you a consultation first, to determine what sort of treatment you require and which oils to use. Essential oils can be used to good effect at home. A few drops of lavender in a bathtub or burner is relaxing, whilst an uplifting blend might include Melissa and Bergamot. Sensual notes can be achieved using Jasmine and Ylang Ylang.

Cranial Sacral Therapy

This is gentle manipulation of bones, usually centred on the skull and spine. The therapist's hands are led to the area that needs work and the body then works to heal itself. Children are especially open to this method of healing, as they haven't yet built up accumulated layers of stress (as many adults have). They have a clearer blueprint of their own health so their bodies are more easily guided back to the state of homeostasis.

Flower Remedies

In the early nineteenth century, Dr. Edward Bach developed a range of flower essences to treat emotional disturbances. This therapy works on a vibrational level, the essence of the plant, its imprint, is captured in water and bottled. Australian and Himalayan bush remedies are also available.

Herbal Medicine

As any herbalist will testify there is a wealth of natural healing properties in the plant kingdom. You can self prescribe for common ailments, but an appointment with a trained medical herbalist is sensible to treat ongoing problems. Whilst traditional Western herbal medicine uses plants commonly found in our gardens or growing wild in the countryside, Chinese herbalism relies on more exotic plants.

Homeopathy

In 1790, a German doctor called Samuel Hahnemann discovered the law of similars and homeopathy was born. He believed that any substance capable of making you ill could also cure you if administered in a small enough dose. A good book on homeopathy can enable you to use this treatment quite safely at home. Andrew Lockie has written several comprehensive books on the subject, *The Family Guide to Homeopathy* (£16.99 Hamish Hamilton) and *The Woman's Guide to Homeopathy* (£16.99 Hamish Hamilton).

Reflexology

A therapy that works on energy zones on the feet (and sometimes hands) which correlate to places on the body. This is a great way to treat people of all ages. You don't need to be a trained reflexologist to give your children the benefits of a treatment at home. Gently stroking your child's foot from toe to heel will have a healing effect.

There are a number of other therapies that can be used to treat the body holistically. Ask friends for recommendations when choosing a practitioner.

Green parenting

Ways to de-stress

It is very important as parents that we look after number one, so that we have the energy to look after others in our family. Here are some ideas for when the going gets tough.

- Wake up early in the morning to enjoy half an hour of quiet time on your own. This will allow you time to collect your thoughts and energise yourself for the day ahead.
- Pull on some wellies and go for a bracing walk. Exercise releases serotonin, the happy hormone, so you start to feel better as soon as you get into your stride.
- Arrange a night in with your partner. Using some sensual essential oils, give each other a massage.
- Breathe properly. Many of us use only a tenth of our lung capacity. Imagine how good we would feel if we learnt to use half or more? Breathwork can teach us how to use more of our lungs' full potential.
- Run a warm bath, surround it with candles, climb in and relax.
- Laugh. Phone a friend who makes you laugh or rent a funny movie.
- Retreat to the garden with a good book.
- Take the kids out for the day. Getting away from the house and the daily routine of chores does everyone the world of good once in a while.
- Take an evening course in something you feel passionate about.
- If all hell is breaking loose and you feel your stress levels rising, walk into another room and count slowly to ten before returning to salvage the situation.
- Remember that tomorrow is another day. If all else fails get an early night and wake up with a fresh take on life.

The importance of exercise

Obesity rates are rising and one in ten six year olds in the UK are now obese. The percentage of children grossly overweight has doubled since 1982 and at the current rate, half of all children could be obese by 2020. So what is the problem and what can we do about it?

Obese children are more likely to suffer from Type II diabetes, when the body stops being able to breakdown sugar and cells are starved of energy. This condition cannot be cured and can lead to complications such as heart disease, nerve damage and blindness. Self-esteem can also be affected, as children who are overweight are often the targets of bullies. Equally, this can cause depression.

The rise in overweight children seems to be linked to people taking less exercise and to the fact that processed foods, containing large amounts of fat, sugars and salt, are more widely available.

Green parenting

We need to encourage good habits in our children today to ensure a healthy adulthood. The two ways to achieve this are by providing a nutritious diet, low in saturated fat, sugar and salt and taking regular exercise as a family. Children need to get at least one hour a day of moderate physical activity and as PE doesn't get the timetable time it deserves in our schools, it figures that parents should be out there getting fit with their kids. The British Heart Foundation suggests brisk walking, swimming, cycling or dancing as activities that could involve the whole family. As many as seven out of ten adults in the UK do not get enough exercise. But regular physical activity lowers blood pressure, reduces the risk of diabetes, helps weight loss and reduces the risk of heart disease and other heart problems. In addition, exercise gives you more energy, greater self-confidence, relief from stress and a lower risk of osteoporosis.

Taking exercise needn't cost a lot of money, you don't need to take out annual gym membership to stay trim. Here are some ways you can beat the bulge on a budget as a family.

- **Take a walk**. Get up earlier and walk to school together. If this isn't possible, plan a walk after school at least three times a week. Get a dog if this helps spur you on

- **Broaden your horizons**. Take up a new activity as a family, be it street dance, jogging or yoga

- **On your bike**. Find out about cycle paths and routes in your area and plan a cycle ride once or twice a week

- **Stay in the UK**. Rather than holidaying abroad, save money and take a trip to one of the UK's areas of natural beauty for a walking, or cycling holiday.

Holistic health

Common childhood ailments and ways to treat them

The most important advice when treating children is to listen to them. Children have an amazing self-preservation instinct and often know exactly what they need to get better. Some children stop eating when they are ill as their bodies need to concentrate on getting well rather than using precious energy to digest food. Other children crave specific foods or can tell you exactly what herb or remedy they need to treat the illness. Listen to your child's advice and you will learn more about their body and what they require.

Chickenpox

Ensure plenty of rest and fluids. Rhus Tox will soothe the skin irritation. Sponge the body with tepid water and add bicarb of soda to the bathwater to ease itching.

Coughs

This is nature's way of clearing an infection of the bronchial passages and protecting the lungs from damage. For this reason, do not suppress a cough. Homeopathic remedy, Bryonia, is effective at treating coughs and is available in pillule or syrup form. Echinacea boosts the immune system. A hot honey and lemon drink can be drunk as often as required. Place a teaspoon of honey and the juice of half a lemon in a cup, fill with boiling water, and allow to cool before drinking.

Colds

This is a natural purification process. If you discourage or suppress, it could carry on in one form or another for many months. Get rest and drink plenty of fluids. Pulsatilla is effective at treating colds with mucus. A honey and lemon drink soothes and cleanses. For extra benefit, steep a small piece of root ginger in the cup which can be removed before serving. Ensure plenty of onions and garlic in the diet.

Croup

Steam inhalation can ease breathing. Spongia is the homeopathic remedy for croup.

Earache

Mullein oil, diluted in a carrier oil, can be dropped into the ear to ease discomfort. Seek the advice of a herbalist. A hot-water bottle placed over the ear can also soothe the pain.

Eczema

When the body cannot eliminate toxins through the usual channels, the lungs, kidneys or liver, the body expels them through the skin. Skin problems such as eczema are the result.

Seek the advice of an alternative practitioner to determine if your child has a problem with the other excretory organs. Avoid petroleum-based products, soaps and scented baby products and do not use detergents or fabric softeners to wash the family's clothes.

Diet can sometimes be the cause. With the help of a nutritionist, try eliminating dairy products from your child's diet and also that of the mother's if breastfeeding. An oat bath will soothe inflamed skin before bed and visualisation can also be beneficial for a good night's sleep. Choose organic cotton clothing, especially for those items worn next to the skin, such as babygrows and underwear.

Fever

Nature's most efficient healing tool. A fever is the body's mechanism for burning up unwanted materials to combat infection. A high temperature is to be encouraged as it is cleaning out the body. However, it is vital to consult a doctor if your newborn baby is running a high temperature or if your child has ingested a poisonous substance.

A dry fever is dangerous but a wet fever heals. Keep your child's fluid intake as high as possible – make sure that you have drinks that they like available. If breastfeeding, allow them to feed for as long and as often as they need. If they

Holistic health

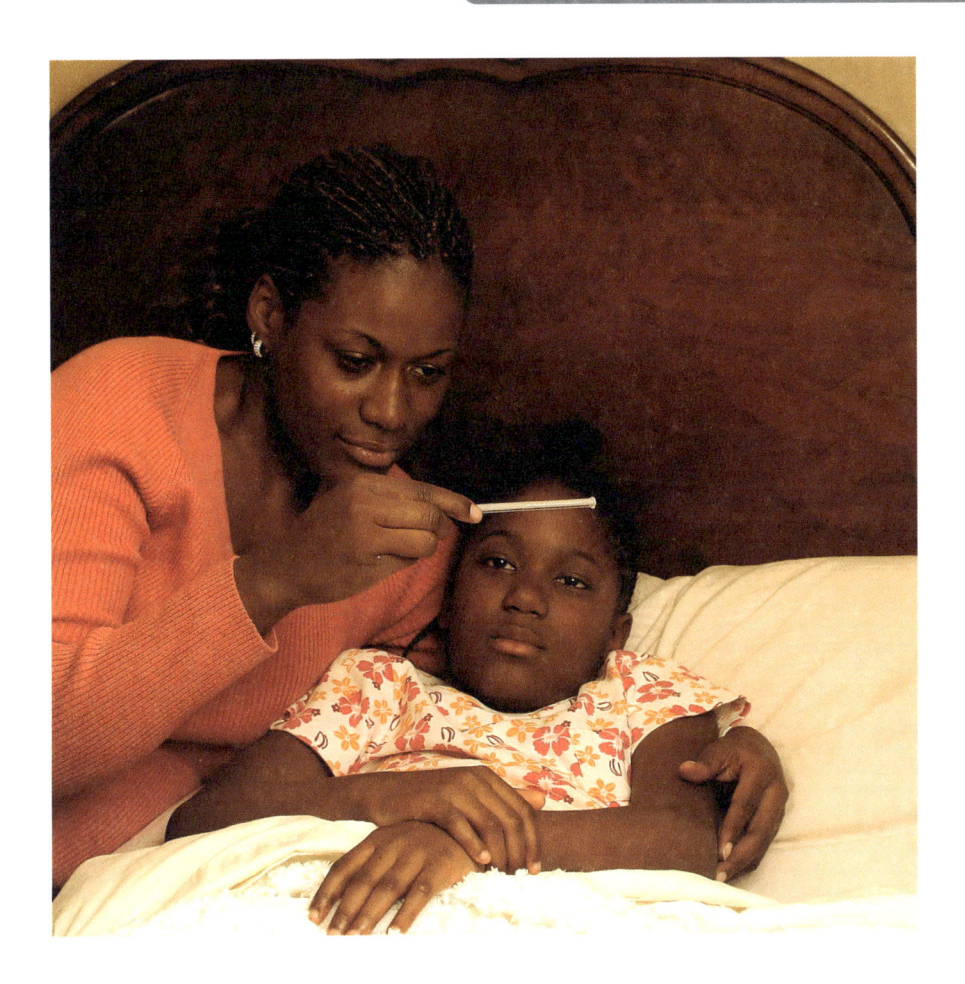

are refusing to drink, run your child a warm bath. Sponge with tepid water afterwards and dress your child in one thin cotton layer. Keep the environment well ventilated. Your child may choose not to eat during the fever.

Make your Own: Rehydration Drink

After diarrhoea, vomiting or during fever this rehydration drink can aid your child's recovery. Place one tablespoon of sugar and one tablespoon of salt in a jug; add 1/2 litre of filtered water and 1 litre of organic apple juice. Encourage your child to drink it throughout the day.

Head lice

Use a herbal shampoo to deter and remove head lice. The most effective treatment is regular brushing with a fine comb. Avoid chemical-based products available in pharmacies, many of which use insecticides that can cause an allergic reaction.

Make your own: Herbal shampoo

Add 5 drops of tea tree, eucalyptus, rosemary and lavender to 100ml of sweet almond oil. Rub into the hair and leave for 12 hours. Wash out and comb thoroughly.

Measles

Ensure time for the child to rest and recuperate. Add a few drops of lavender oil to cool water and sponge down. See advice for fever.

Nappy Rash

Allow plenty of nappy-free time, and apply calendula ointment to soothe sore skin. Refrain from using perfumed wipes, which can be a harsh irritant to delicate skin. Use a cotton flannel soaked in warm water instead.

Sore throat

Sage or thyme tea can be made with honey to soothe a sore throat. The homeopathic remedy Heper Sulp can be used.

Make your own: Cough medicine

Place half an onion cut into rings into a shallow dish. Cover with honey and leave to infuse overnight. In the morning, strain and bottle the resulting liquid. This makes an effective syrup for sore throats, coughs and colds.

Teething

Homeopathic remedies, chamomilla and Pulsatilla are recommended. Amber is a natural analgesic. A necklace can be bought to ease teething discomfort.

Holistic health

Immunity and vaccinations

The Vaccination Debate

In this country, there is an immunisation programme that covers children from 2 months old up to teenagers of 14. During this time, children receive inoculations against a number of serious diseases including mumps, measles, meningitis, diphtheria and polio. It is believed that this will give immunity to the diseases vaccinated against and it is reckoned to have eliminated the most harmful and fatal diseases from the UK that were once common. In brief, this works by injecting a weak form of the disease into the child's bloodstream. The body then creates antibodies to fight the disease, the blueprint of which remains in the body ready to fight off any future attacks.

Until quite recently, it was very difficult to find any information about the alternatives to vaccination. Indeed today, the NHS offers little or no advice to parents who are unsure about subjecting their children to this programme. Instead, millions of pounds are spent each year on advertising campaigns to encourage parents to have their child immunised.

Fortunately there are now groups and organisations that are raising awareness about the other side of the story, offering parents the chance to make an informed decision about whether or not they follow the Government's recommended vaccination programme. And in the UK, we are fortunate enough to have a choice. In some countries the vaccinations are compulsory.

Those experts that are anti-vaccination state that the reason why fatal diseases have all but been eradicated in this country is due to the improvements in living conditions over the last century. Certainly, we now benefit from cleaner streets, properly sanitised water systems and better levels of hygiene. It is also pointed out that in injecting a disease into the bloodstream you are effectively bypassing the body's usual line of defence. Our bodies are used to dealing with infections that enter via our mouths; air borne disease. The antibodies stimulated by the

Holistic Health

> ## To help you to make a decision:
> - Research as much as possible (see directory at the back)
> - Talk to your partner, health visitor, friends and homeopath about immunisation. Discuss your concerns
> - Make your own list of the pros and cons for each side after reading and talking about it. Write this list down so that you can refer back and add to it as you discover new information

jab are different to those that our bodies would create if fighting disease naturally. So, they would say, it is questionable how effective these manufactured antibodies would be anyhow when faced with a real infection.

Many people believe that vaccinations compromise the individual's immune system. A baby of two months has not had the chance to build up a strong immune system so the three vaccinations that are supposed to take place at two, four and six months of age are placing a real strain on the baby's immature system.

Another issue that arises is the fact that whilst immunisation may protect against acute disease, chronic illnesses are believed to often develop as a result. These include, eczema, asthma, diabetes, allergies and autism. Many parents attribute their child's autism or allergies to the MMR (Mumps, Measles and Rubella) vaccine.

If you do decide to vaccinate your children, you might consider waiting until your baby is older, when their immune system is more mature and able to cope better. If your baby is unwell, postpone the vaccination.

Do not feel pressurised into making a decision. It is an important choice and one that must not be taken lightly. Some medical professionals are so convinced of the benefits of vaccinations that it can feel like you are being bamboozled into having your child immunised. Green Parenting is not, however, about giving a definitive answer on these debates. Its purpose is to draw parents attention to them so that they can make an informed decision on the matter.

Green parenting

If you choose not to vaccinate your child it is a good idea to boost their immune system using natural methods.

1. Eat a healthy organic wholefood diet

2. Let them eat dirt. Don't be afraid of dirt and germs – they are vital for our children to build a healthy immune system

3. Make time for illness – when your children are ill, be there for them. Support and nurture them and use natural remedies to treat their ailments. Don't suppress the illness, it's more than likely to materialise as another illness later on!

4. Spend as much time as possible outside. Physical exercise and a daily dose of sunlight is vital for growing children (and adults)

5. Seek the advice of a homeopath or alternative practitioner

6. Cut down on sugar, or cut it out of your children's diet altogether. There are natural alternatives such as fructose and molasses that can be used, although you will have to be very label conscious as there is sugar in most packaged food from bread and crisps to drinks and cereals. Sugar stops the immune system from functioning properly

7. Breastfeed for as long as possible. Breast milk offers huge amounts of protective antibodies

5

Green education

Green parenting

Teaching children about the environment

It is important that our children are aware of environmental damage and the steps we can take to prevent it. We must teach them how to look after the planet for a sustainable future and one way to do this is to encourage a child's natural fascination with the world around them.

Environmental education can seem like a fairly heavy area to get into with a child, but this need not be the case. In fact, studying our environment can be both entertaining and engaging. Starting at home, parents can set a good example by recycling and composting as much waste as possible. The thought of worms munching their way through your leftovers will probably be an exciting prospect for most children. Loading up the recycling boxes can be an enjoyable weekly job. Looking after the wildlife in your back garden or local park can make green issues more accessible for children. Providing bug homes, bird boxes, toad hideaways, a butterfly garden or food for other wildlife during the winter months are all important projects that children can organise and get involved in.

Water conservation is another issue that you can teach at home. Encourage children to turn off the tap when brushing their teeth and explain why showers are better than baths. Energy conservation can be a useful learning tool too. Teach your children to switch off lights when they leave a room, put on a sweater when cold rather than turning on the heating and avoid battery powered toys.

You may like to join a conservation group such as The Wildlife Trusts or the RSPB as a family to benefit from activities and events specifically geared towards children. This allows you to meet other families interested in conservation and encourages you and your children to get involved on a local level in projects that improve your community.

Green education

Fun and free activities for families

Playtime can be packed with exciting games that don't cost a penny and help to protect the environment. Read on to find the projects best suited to your child's age.

For babies:

- **Make a mobile** out of unwanted CDs and hang it in the window so that it catches the light

- **Get together with other parents and start a music group.** Babies love listening to their mother's voice, and it is the first sound that they recognise

- **Don't worry about buying expensive toys**. A baby will delight in the contents of your cupboards and cutlery drawer. Provide some saucepans and wooden spoons for musical entertainment

- **Take a walk in the park**. Nestled close to their mother's chest in a carrier, your baby will enjoy a walk in the fresh air. It is a chance to watch everything happening around them from a safe cosy place

- **Make a tactile cloth book using scraps of fabric**, cut to a similar size and sewn together down one edge

- **A baby massage** is a wonderful loving way to end the day

- **Action rhymes and peek-a-boo games** will delight babies from a young age

- **A game of skittles** can be made by placing a few handfuls of sand in the bottom of six empty plastic water bottles. You and your baby can take turns trying to knock them down using a tennis ball.

Green parenting

For Toddlers:

- **Go for an adventure walk**. Take a walk around your local neighbourhood with all your senses on alert. What sounds can you hear? What sights can you see?

- **Have a crawling race**

- **Make a house or a shop out of a large cardboard box**. You could create an elaborate play space with fabric curtains and pretend food or keep it simple and just cut a hole in the box to make a door

- **Start a scrapbook**. Staple several pieces of scrap paper together to make a book. Collect a pile of magazines, a pair of scissors and a pot of glue and get cutting and sticking

- **Make some playdough**
  What you need:

1/2 cup salt	1 cup flour	1 tablespoon cream of tartar
1 tablespoon oil	1 cup water	

  Place all the ingredients in a heavy-based pan over a low to medium heat. Stir constantly until the dough comes together in a ball in the centre of the pan. Allow to cool before giving to your children

- **Create a dressing-up box.** Place old scraps of fabric, unwanted hats, shoes and jewellery in a large cardboard box for your children to use

- **Water play.** Fill a washing up bowl with warm water. Place on the floor on some towels and give your toddler some bottles, containers, corks and bottle tops to play with

- **Make some musical instruments.** Shakers can be created by placing dried beans inside a sealed container, guitars by stretching rubber bands over a shoe box, and panpipes by taping different lengths of drinking straw together.

Green education

For 5 to 8 year olds:

- **Hold a concert.** Choose some of your favourite music or make your own. Dancing and microphones optional!

- **Go for a nature walk.** Before you set out think about some of the wildlife you might spot and make a note of any unusual species that you find. Your children might like to have a notebook especially for this purpose

- **Have a themed family evening.** Choose an era or a country and work together to create a themed meal. You could even dress up, make menu cards and find music and games to play, specific to your chosen country

- **Start a vegetable plot.** Dig over an area of your garden. It needn't be big; an area of 2m2 is enough to grow a few staples such as salad crops

- **Get recycling.** Kids love sorting things out and getting involved in household duties. Encourage them to sort out paper, cardboard, plastic and cans into different boxes ready for recycling day

- **Make your own paper** using scrap paper and even flowers and leaves. Find instructions on the internet

- **Find out how to attract more wildlife into your garden,** either by planting specific plants or by putting up butterfly, bat or bird boxes and leaving out bird food. A simple insect box can be made by gathering a bundle of twigs and bamboo (about 30 cm long), tying with string and hanging from a tree. Insects will make their homes in the hollows

- **Play charades.** Kids of this age love to play this guessing game

Green parenting

For older children:

- **Create a pond**. A garden pond can be as big or small as you want it. Even a 1m2 site will host a variety of pond life. Get your children involved in planning, digging, lining, sourcing local water plants and maintaining it. Projects like this can enhance a child's sense of self-esteem, as the end result is so enjoyable for the whole family

- **Grow a tree**. Planting an acorn in the autumn and tending it for years to come can be an important lesson in patience!

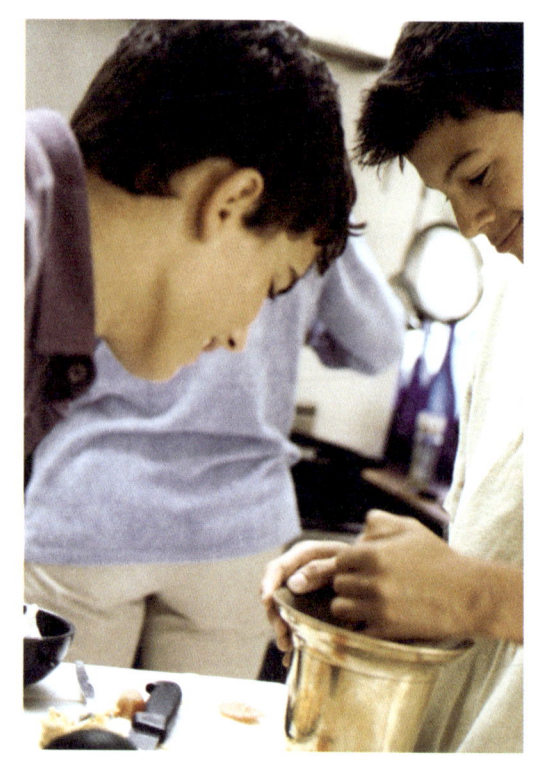

- **Play team games** such as football, hockey, and basketball. Is there an area where local children can get together for a game?

- **Create a family scrapbook**. Interview family members, take silly photos and draw pictures. These can be compiled into a wonderful memento. Another fun book to create as a family is a cookbook containing recipes handed down through the generations

- **Keep chickens**. A great introduction to self-sustainability, chickens make fascinating and amusing pets and you get a steady supply of eggs

- **Get cooking together**. On birthdays and special occasions plan a meal that can be cooked and shared as a family

- **Organise a regular family night.** Sunday is a good bet because everyone is usually relaxed and it is a pleasant start to the week. This could be a board game and cocoa evening, a chance for a fire and storytelling or a movies and popcorn night.

Green toys

What could be more natural than playing with toys? Unfortunately, some toys contain hidden nasties that can cause serious health defects in our children.

Soft PVC toys can contain phthalates (toxic chemicals) that can leach out and be ingested when sucked or chewed.

Although toys intended for the mouth containing soft PVCs have been removed from the market, babies are not particularly discerning about what they put in their mouth so it is possible that they could still come into contact with these toxic chemicals. Given that phthalates have been found to cause liver, kidney and reproductive problems, it may be better to avoid soft PVC toys altogether.

Of course, plastic toys are also detrimental to the environment, releasing toxic chemicals into the atmosphere during manufacture. Not to mention the short shelf life of the majority of plastic playthings which break easily, often require batteries and end up clogging up landfill sites.

Fortunately, there is now a good choice of alternative playthings for your little one. Choose wooden and fabric toys. If possible ensure that the wood is from a sustainable source and that soft toys are created using 100 percent organic cotton. Another benefit of these natural toys is that they have great longevity and can be passed down to the next generation. Fair trade toys are becoming more widely available. Purchasing these for your child ensures that the producer has been paid a good wage and that no child labour is involved. A delightful selection of dolls, jigsaws, play scenes and characters can be found at specialist shops and on the internet.

There seems to be something of a craft revolution happening at the moment. It has become cool to knit and make your own clothes. Creating toys for your children can be great fun, therapeutic and rewarding. You may choose to make your own soft toys from organic fabric or perhaps wooden blocks from well-sanded off-cuts.

Green parenting

It's in the box:

Every parent knows that the box a toy comes in is more interesting than the toy itself. So take this concept a step further and give your child a box as a present. You could customise the gift by including some paints so that your child can decorate the box and turn it into a play space, or include some old clothes, such as hats, dresses, jackets and costume jewellery for a special dressing up box. It is now possible to buy recycled cardboard toys for eco-youngsters such as castles, space ships and children's furniture. See the directory for more information.

The effect of TV

Teachers have cited that TV kills creativity and disrupts concentration. Now parents are finding out themselves as our electronic media gets ever more invasive. Many agree that TV induces cognitive passivity, deadens imagination and displaces opportunities for play and social interaction.

Children who watch TV regularly spend up to 2 months per year glued to the box. When a child reaches the age of six they may have spent a year of their life in front of the television set.

This is a shocking amount of time spent inert and vulnerable to the powers of advertising and branding. But what can we do about it? Here are some tips to living without a TV or cutting down the amount of viewing time in your family.

Green education

Ways to live without a TV

- Don't have a TV set in the house in the first place. If your child grows up in a house with no TV, but plenty of other interesting activities, growing up without it is unlikely to be an issue.

- Cover up or hide it away. Having to drag the TV out of the loft every time the kids want to watch a programme will make everyone think twice about switching it on.

- Have a TV free holiday. When you get back perhaps you'll feel inspired to watch less and live more.

- If you can manage a week or a month without watching TV observe your children's behaviour during the trial. Do they spend more time playing outside? Playing creatively? Reading books? Talking to you? Do they have more patience, more energy and less desire for junk food? These are all physical and behavioural traits that researchers and teachers have observed in children whose families have 'switched off'.

What are the other benefits to living without a TV?

- **More family time,** a chance to really interact with each other, play games, go for a walk
- **Better relationships** – adults who don't switch on the TV in the evening when the kids have gone to bed have a chance to talk and listen to each other
- **Less desire for material possessions.** Those advertising executives aren't stupid. No matter how savvy we think we are, advertising on TV is a powerful tool in dictating which brand we choose or how we spend our money. Think of the effect on kids who don't have the experience to understand that material goods cannot bring happiness
- **Longer attention spans.** Televisual viewing sets children up to expect rapidly changing visuals and sounds. If the rest of life doesn't live up to these expectations they can soon become bored and that leads to frustration and behavioural issues
- **A family of individuals.** TV is a powerful anti-socialiser. Get rid of it and children are better able to be themselves and actualise their individuality
- **A chance to enjoy books.** Books, unlike TV, can be chosen according to your child's mood or frame of mind. They encourage a child's imagination and can be a shared or solitary experience
- **Greater creativity.** By taking away the box that fills spare time you are encouraging your family to find other pursuits to occupy their time. Children who don't watch TV have a more vivid imagination and greater social skills
- **More money.** If you take into account all the purchases your family makes as a result of televisual viewing you will probably make considerable savings over a year. Add to that the cost of a licence and you are one step closer to that dream holiday.

Alternative education

More and more families are questioning our current school system and opting for an alternative education for their children. These are some of the options available to children outside of mainstream schooling:

Home Education

Thousands of families in the UK choose home education, where children learn at home rather than at school. Many choose autonomous education; child-led learning whereby the child chooses when and what to learn. Some families reconstruct school in their home with a fixed timetable, but others celebrate the freedom that home education offers and enjoy watching their child learning at his/her own pace. Home education really starts the moment a baby is born. As parents we guide them in learning to talk and walk; they are constantly discovering new skills and exploring. A home-educated child continues in much the same way. Studies have concluded that home-educated children are usually more advanced, socially and intellectually, in comparison to school children. They mix with a much wider age range of children, as well as adults, and get involved in much more hands on learning.

Forest Schools

This is a school set up to encourage children to take an interest and active participation in outdoor life and nature. It is based on inspiring and challenging children and encouraging a greater sense of self-esteem through completing tasks in a woodland environment. All ages can benefit from this style of education. In Denmark, the Forest School forms a full-time learning experience for the child. Forest Schools in the UK are set up as a part-time resource to be used by local schools and education groups.

Montessori Education

Maria Montessori was born in Italy in 1870 and having trained as a doctor she worked with mentally and socially handicapped children. Her work led her to develop her own theories about education. She believed that children learned best on their own and working at their own pace. From her beliefs and working experience, the Montessori method was born and it is now practised in schools worldwide. A Montessori classroom is set up with activities that the children can choose as they please. Emphasis is placed on everyday skills and children are offered scaled-down versions of adult tools to work with. Teachers do not teach, rather they 'direct' the child's learning and development.

Steiner Waldorf Method

Steiner Waldorf education focuses on natural development, creativity and learning at the child's pace. Formal education does not start until the age of seven, when it is believed they are naturally ready for that kind of work. This method is based upon the teachings of Rudolph Steiner, who believed that play is the most important work a child can do. A Steiner school is often homely and has toys made from natural materials, in muted colours, to encourage imaginative play. No artificial materials or colours are likely to be found there. Steiner believed that we are all rhythmical beings and emphasis is placed on the changing of the seasons within the Steiner classroom. A seasonal table marks the changes in nature and songs and routines mark the passing of time on a daily basis.

A day in the life of a home educating family

"We wake early and head out to feed the chickens. They certainly don't like being shut in their hen house after it gets light. Sometimes, we climb back into bed with a pile of books to enjoy before breakfast. Jazzie, six, has taught herself to read in the last year and she likes to share her skills with friends and family. Today she reads a Dr. Seuss book to us all. She reads with real verve and passion. I believe this is because she learnt to read when she was ready and the words hold a real importance for her. Recently, she has branched out to include non-fiction books in her repertoire, especially science books and those explaining how our bodies work.

After a family breakfast of porridge, fruit, toast and smoothies, we set out for our weekly home education group. This is a group of families with children aged from one to nine, who get together for just one day a week. However, lots of other opportunities arise during the week to spend time with other children and adults. We might organise a picnic and a nature walk, a visit to the local museum or a creative afternoon at a friend's house.

Green parenting

Our regular meet is loosely structured and has a theme that changes every session. This week we are exploring sound and the session involves science experiments, singing songs, making and playing musical instruments and creating sound stories. We share lunch and catch up with our friends – it really is a diverse group of people, but we agree on the principles of home education for our children. No child is coerced into taking part if they don't want to. Respect for others is key to the functioning of the group and difficult issues are dealt with gently and with adult support.

Home educating for us means family learning; we are all discovering and learning together. I do not think of myself as my children's teacher, rather I am a facilitator and I offer the educational experiences that I think they need, when they are ready.

On the way home, we visit the library and take out the maximum number of books. Daisy is four and frustrated that she can't read yet, but she loves books and has a great stash under her bed for early morning entertainment. Then we go for a romp in the woods near our house before tea. Jazzie and Daisy climb trees and I hunt for mushrooms under the leafy carpet of the woods. Whilst rooting around we talk about subjects ranging from why people shoot pheasants to how rain is created. A lot of our discoveries start this way, we will have a conversation and be prompted to follow the subject up in a book or on the internet. Before we know it, we have a project on our hands. This seems to be true for most of the home educating families that I know. Conversations inspire much of the learning which takes place.

Children ask questions incessantly until they start school. Suddenly, upon entering the school system they stop. I believe this is because in a class of thirty children, there is no one available to answer their questions any more so their inquisitiveness becomes suppressed. Also, the National Curriculum and battery of tests and exams our children are subjected to do not encourage free thinkers. They leave room for only one correct answer and way of doing things. Children can have their individuality squashed out of them at school if they are not careful (or very robust).

Back home we make tea together - an omelette using our chickens' eggs. Jazzie chops vegetables and Daisy lays the table. We all eat together and then play a game by the fire before easing ourselves into the bedtime routine. Both girls are

Green parenting

very creative and in addition to painting and drawing they spend a lot of time role-playing. They act out familiar stories with their toys or become the characters themselves. One of our favourites is Mr and Mrs Bombay Mix, a crazy couple with fifty children, although Poochie always has me in stitches too. He is one of Jazzie's characters, a sort of lounging youth, who likes fishing and playing football and speaks in an impossibly gruff voice for a six year old.

After the requisite bedtime story each, Jazzie will continue to read for an hour or so before sleeping, Daisy will ensure all her dolls are comfortable with blankets and pillows before dropping off herself. And then it's downstairs to enjoy a little adult-time curled up by the fire, listening to music and maybe enjoying a (purely medicinal) glass of red wine."

6

The natural home

Green parenting

With rates of allergies and asthma on the rise, the chemicals in our home have come under closer scrutiny and there are more and more companies offering environmentally-friendly products for the home.

When decorating your home choose natural paints, which are unlikely to contain Volatile Organic Compounds (VOCs), carbon based chemicals that easily evaporate into the air and can act as irritants or carcinogens. Natural or green paints are made from ingredients like plants, chalk and linseed oil. You may find that they take longer to dry than regular paints, but the extra time that you invest is worth it when you consider that you're safeguarding your family's health. Choose organic cotton or hemp for soft furnishings and bedding. Environmentally, non-organic cotton is the world's most destructive crop. Twelve

The natural home

percent of pesticides and 26 percent of the world's insecticide use is for growing cotton. Forty percent of cotton grown in the States is genetically modified and the products are often dyed with toxic chemicals and treated with flame retardant formaldehyde. The production of cotton also requires huge amounts of water - often not something which is in great abundance in the countries where it is produced.

Laminated wood, chipboard or MDF also leach chemicals that are harmful to the respiratory system. Furniture made from chipboard releases formaldehyde into the atmosphere, a known carcinogen. Choose non-treated furniture made with hardwood from sustainable sources. But, be aware that getting hardwood from sustainable sources can be difficult and its FSC (Forest Stewardship Council) labelling is not always legitimate.

When purchasing a mattress ask the retailer whether it has been treated with flame retardants or stain repellents.

Green parenting

The natural home

Chemicals in your home
– potential problems and alternatives

Kitchen

Product:	Contains:	Problems:	Alternatives:
Multi purpose cleaning products	Phthalates	Widespread contaminates, some of which may cause liver, liver kidney and testicular damage	Home-made natural cleaners
	Artificial Musks	Absorbed through skin and found in breast milk, fatty tissue and blood. May cause liver damage and interfere with brain messages	
	Alkyphenols	(Nonylphenol, nonyphenol etnoxylate, alkylphenol, alkylphenol etnoxylate). Can disrupt sperm production and damage body's abilities to fight germs	
	Endocrine Disrupters	Can cause birth defects, abnormalities in the reproductive system and disrupt the body's natural chemical messages	
Laundry Detergent	Artificial Musks	Absorbed through skin and found in breast milk, fatty tissue and blood. May cause liver damage and interfere with brain messages	Soap nuts or Eco balls

Bathroom

Product:	Contains:	Problems:	Alternatives:
Toilet Cleaner	Ammonium Compounds, Sodium bi-sulphate, oxalic acid and muriatic acids	Can cause burns, skin irritation, and respiratory problems	Home-made natural cleaner
Shampoo	Phthalaltes	Widespread contaminates some of which may cause liver, kidney and testicular damage	Shampoos made from natural ingredients

Green parenting

Bathroom continued...

Product:	Contains:	Problems:	Alternatives:
Deodorant	Artificial Musks	Absorbed through skin and found in breast milk, fatty tissue and blood. May cause liver damage and interfere with brain messages	Naturally-made deodorants
	Aluminium compounds	There have been claims that these can cause breast cancer, but there has been no scientific evidence to verify this.	
	Artificial Musks	Absorbed through skin and found in breast milk, fatty tissue and blood. May cause liver damage and interfere with brain messages	
Vinyl flooring	Phthalates	Widespread contaminates some of which may cause liver, kidney and testicular damage	Wood, cork or ceramic tiles. However, wood and cork will probably be secured down by a formaldehyde backing glue and will need to be varnished. Ceramic tiles will need some kind of cement which is not necessarily dangerous, but will probably contain some nasty chemicals.
	Chlorinated Paraffin	Some are category three carcinogens; meaning they may cause cancer	
	Organotins	Very poisonous, can attack the immune system, cause birth defects and attack neurons in the brain	

Living room

Product:	Contains:	Problems:	Alternatives:
Air Freshener	Pthalates	Widespread contaminates some of which may cause liver, kidney and testicular damage	Essential oils and fresh air.
	Artificial Musks	Absorbed through skin and found in breast milk fatty tissue and blood. May cause liver damage and interfere with brain messages	
Furniture Polish	Ammonia, petroleum, distillates	Affects respiratory system	Beeswax

The natural home

Product:	Contains:	Problems:	Alternatives:
Carpets	Brominated flame retardants	Exposure in the womb has been shown to interfere with brain development in animals. No data on human babies yet	Floorboards or natural flooring
	Organotins	Very poisonous, can attack the immune system, cause birth defects and attack neurons in the brain	
	Endocrine Disrupters	Can cause birth defects, abnormalities in the reproductive system and disrupt the body's natural chemical messages	

Bedroom

Product:	Contains:	Problems:	Alternatives:
Paint	Alkyphenols	(Nonylphenol, nonyphenol etnoxylate, alkylphenol, alkylphenol etnoxylate). Can disrupt sperm production and damage body's abilities to fight germs	Natural paints, although not chemical-free, offer a safer alternative
	Endocrine Disruptors	Can cause birth defects abnormalities in the reproductive system and disrupt the body's natural chemical messages	
Wallpaper	Fungicides	Emit fumes that contribute to indoor air pollution	Natural paints, although not chemical-free, do offer a safer alternative
MDF furniture	Adhesives Formaldehyde	Affects respiratory system	Hardwood furniture from a sustainable source, although more difficult to obtain, is a viable alternative.
Bedding	Brominated flame retardants	As above (carpets)	Organic cotton bedding is a safer alternative.
	Organotins	As above (carpets)	
	Endocrine Disrupters	As above (carpets)	

Green parenting

What to use for a naturally clean home

- Lemon is a natural bleach. The juice of a lemon can be applied to stubborn stains on clothes to help clean them
- Bicarbonate of soda has many uses. An open pot in the fridge absorbs nasty odours. To clean a dirty oven sprinkle over the base, cover with vinegar and leave for an hour before wiping down
- Vinegar can also be used to clean windows. Dilute 25ml of vinegar with half a litre of water in a spray bottle
- Lavender essential oil makes an excellent fabric freshener in the conditioner drawer of the washing machine
- Beeswax polish can be used to give a healthy shine to wooden floors and furniture
- Soap nuts, a biodegradable alternative to laundry detergents, are grown in India and Nepal and harvested sustainably. They contain saponin, a natural soap and can also be boiled up to create a cleaning liquid that can be used on the oven, car or anything else that needs cleaning
- Vinegar is an effective loo cleaner. Pour into the toilet and leave overnight. Flush away in the morning for a sparkling bowl.

A natural home

We all need somewhere calm to retreat to at the end of a busy day. A home should be a place that replenishes the soul and reflects who you are. You will also find that your home reflects how you feel, which is why it is a good idea to keep it free from clutter and extraneous junk. An untidy home makes for a cluttered mind.

Green parenting

Ten ways to create a healthy living environment:

1 Open the windows. Throw open the windows every morning and allow the fresh air to circulate. Electrical equipment releases VOCs into the air when they are on. This can irritate our respiratory system, but fresh air clears out the majority of these fumes. Hoovering is also effective

2 Buy a spider plant. Plants have been found to have air purification properties. Peace lilies, weeping figs, bamboo, spider plants and golden pathos are some of the best varieties for clearing toxins

3 Chuck out any chemical cleaners. Use natural cleaning products instead. They are cheaper, in most cases more effective, and don't have an impact on the environment.

4 Get the chi flowing. Basic Feng Shui can be easily applied to your home. Don't crowd your space with too much furniture, choose pieces with rounded edges, use mirrors to reflect light in dark spaces and remember that plants, crystals and wind chimes can all encourage good energy flow

5 Let the light shine on. Natural light nurtures physical wellbeing, so encourage as much sunlight into your home as possible by avoiding heavy dark curtains and keeping your space uncluttered. Consider installing skylights or a sun pipe to bring light into dark rooms

6 Colour me beautiful. Consider how different colours affect your moods before choosing your décor. Colour therapists suggest the following:
- Pink for a baby or child's room as it is soothing and nurturing. It helps to dissolve anger and encourages unconditional love

- Yellow for hallways as it promotes feelings of confidence and stimulates mental activity

- Indigos, blues and greens for bedrooms as this end of the spectrum is calming and relaxing

- Red for a dining area as it stimulates the appetite

- Orange for living rooms and creative space, as it is the colour of sociability and is warming and energizing

7 Sort out those ions. Fluorescent lighting, TV and computer screens, electrical equipment and man-made fibres all emit positive ions, upsetting the balance in the home and causing anxiety, depression and migraines. Negative ions make us feel good and you can replenish them by investing in an ionizer, which cleans the air of dust, pollen, fumes and dirt.

8 Sweetly scented. Aromatherapy can be used in the home to lift the spirits, increase productivity or calm and soothe the inhabitants. Use an oil burner or an ioniser with a blend of your favourite essential oils

9 Avoid EMFs where possible. Electromagnetic fields are emitted by electrical equipment. Cover screens and switch off computers when not in use. Look out for eco-gadgets such as wind up radios and alarm clocks and solar powered equipment to use as alternatives. The Bio-Shield is a small device that protects against the energy waves emitted by computers and mobile phones

10 Get natural. When decorating, consider using natural paints rather than conventional paints that contain toxic chemicals and wallpaper that often contains fungicides. Choose wooden floorboards or natural materials such as coir, cork or jute rather than carpets or laminate flooring, which can leach formaldehyde into the atmosphere.

Green parenting

Energy conservation

There are many ways to cut energy use in the home that will save you money as well as reduce the impact on the environment.

First of all, be conscious of wasting energy. Fix that dripping tap; when using the kettle don't boil more water than you need and place lids on saucepans when cooking. Remember to switch appliances off when not in use and close the curtains at dusk to stop heat from escaping through the windows.

In the winter you could choose to put on a sweater and turn your thermostat down by 1°C. This could shave £30 off your annual heating bill. Energy saving light bulbs last up to 12 times longer than ordinary bulbs and will save you around £78 per bulb over their lifetime.

Because around 40 per cent of heat loss in a typical home is through the walls and the loft, it's worth checking whether yours are insulated. Insulating cavity walls and the loft can significantly reduce the utility bills, especially when combined with draught proofing, tank and pipe insulation and double-glazing. Your local council may offer grants for insulation.

There is also funding and advice for those who want to consider renewable energy systems for their home. You can choose from biomass, which provides heating for the home by burning woodchips or similar substances in a stove; a small scale wind generator, which harnesses the wind's energy to convert into electricity; a micro hydro plant, which generates electricity from flowing water, even a small stream; or solar energy, which can be channelled using photovoltaic cells, usually positioned on the roof to capture maximum sunlight and create electricity. More information about these systems and the grants available can be found at www.est.org.uk or tel: 0800 298 3978.

Organic gardening

Over three quarters of us are committed to organic gardening. Recent research by the Royal Horticultural Society found that 75% of gardeners between 15 and 34 refuse to use any pesticides on their garden. This adherence to chemical-free gardening methods creates not only a haven for wildlife, but for gardeners too. They can appreciate an outside space humming with insects and prolific with home-grown produce.

In the UK, our 15 million gardens cover about 270,000 hectares. This is a huge area that can play an important part in wildlife conservation especially when habitat loss and climate change are a real threat to biodiversity. You can encourage wildlife by creating the right conditions in your garden with a few easy steps. For organic gardening guides go to www.impactpublishing.co.uk.

Green parenting

How to create an eco-friendly garden

- Compost as much kitchen waste as possible. A wormery will take cooked food as well as kitchen scraps, cardboard and other waste. This nutrient rich substance can then be used all over your garden to improve soil conditions

- Leave piles of wood for hibernating creatures

- Plant a tree or two. If you have the space, introduce some of the UK's ancient apple varieties. They will yield fruit for the family and neighbours and will support a large number of insects, in turn providing food for birds and animals

- Choose hedges rather than fences. Berry producing shrubs provide food for the birds in the winter as well as a home for a myriad of other creatures

- If you have the space, plant a wildflower meadow. Not only is our native meadowland beautiful, but it also encourages butterflies, bees and other insects

- Create a pond. An old sink will do, submerged and planted up with native water plants, ideally without fish. Sit back and wait for the aquatic creatures to move in

- Leave seed heads to provide food for birds and other creatures during the winter months.

The natural home

Green parenting

Gardening with kids

You don't need a huge amount of space to create a garden that's full of sensory delights for children. Above all, the most important thing is to let them join in and get their hands dirty. Teaching your children how to tend a garden and grow their own food could be one of the most vital skills they learn.

- Place bird and bat boxes in the trees in your garden to encourage roosting

- Grow tasty plants such as strawberries, beans, herbs and nasturtiums that children can pick and eat straightaway

- Allow your child their own plot where they can experiment. They may want to turn it into a muddy excavation site for their toy cars and diggers or perhaps they'll choose to plant rows of pretty flowers. It boosts their self-esteem to be given free-reign on their own patch. And experimenting with soil or growing flowers are useful learning tools for later projects

- Borrow inspirational books about children and their gardens from the library. Try *Willie's Garden, Grow Organic, Eat Organic* and *Oliver's Vegetables*

- Grow useful plants such as lavender that can be used to make herbal sachets and herbs such as lemon balm that can be used in salads

- Plants that smell divine like jasmine are another winner for children

- Buy your child some scaled-down tools and gardening gloves to make tending to their patch easier

- Make time for family outings to famous gardens such as the Garden Organic (HDRA) gardens, RBG Kew or National Trust properties. It's a wonderful opportunity for children to let off steam and get a sense of the awesome creativity that goes into developing such a space.

7

50 ways to be a green parent

50 ways to be a green parent

1. Give lots of love. You can never spoil a child with too many hugs or kisses

2. Buy organic food from local sources. See www.whyorganic.org for your nearest box scheme or farmers market

3. Cook your own food where possible and avoid processed foods

4. Choose second-hand clothes for your children, if you buy new, choose fair-trade and/or organic

5. Avoid parabens and SLS. Parabens are synthetic preservatives found in most bodycare products. They are derived from petro-chemicals and are easily absorbed into the skin. They have been shown to disrupt hormone activity and cause skin irritation. SLS stands for Sodium Lauryl Sulphate, a detergent that is rapidly absorbed by the body and retained in the body's organs. Use natural body care products, organic if possible

6. DON'T use a microwave. Food cooked in a microwave can contain higher levels of free radicals, potentially cancer causing compounds. It also affects the natural energy levels of foods

7. Recycle household waste. See www.wastewatch.org.uk for local recycling info

8. Give unwanted goods to charity or pass onto friends and family

9. Get freecycling. See www.freecycle.com

10. Leave the car at home and walk instead. Its good for your health, pocket and environment

50 ways to be a green parent

11 Switch to a green energy supplier.
- See www.greenelectricity.co.uk to find out more

12 Choose wooden floors over carpets

13 Make your garden wildlife-friendly

14 Become vegetarian or eat less meat. If you do eat meat make sure it is organic

15 Refuse plastic bags, choose cotton instead

16 Ditch the TV or cut down on family viewing time. Play board games, talk and tell stories instead

17 Share family meals as often as possible

18 Avoid conventional cleaning products. Try using natural substitutes instead

19 Teach your children about green issues

20 Include super foods in your diet wherever possible

21 Breastfeed for as long as you can

22 Eat locally grown seasonal foods

23 Get composting

24 Use holistic medicine to treat family illness

25 Get a bus pass

50 ways to be a green parent

26 Read to your children

27 Buy organic underwear for you and your kids

28 Choose wooden and natural toys

29 Read up on the debates over vaccinations before making a decision about your children

30 Reduce sugar in your family's diet

31 Grow your own vegetables

32 Spend more time with your kids

33 Respect your children

34 Choose a sling instead of a buggy

35 If possible have a natural home birth rather than risk the medical intervention of a hospital birth

36 Enjoy daily quiet periods together as a family

37 Allow your children to express themselves freely. Be wary of bottling up emotions yourself

38 Listen to your children.

39 Get creative. Celebrate the turning of the seasons and family birthdays with great flamboyance

40 Search out and spend time with other families who share similar ethics and beliefs

50 ways to be a green parent

Get out and experience nature everyday	**41**
Use ecoballs or soap nuts for your family's laundry	**42**
Make time for yourself regularly	**43**
Make time for your relationship with your partner	**44**
Boost your child's immune system with a good diet, plenty of love and fresh air	**45**
Boost your child's self-esteem by showing love and setting boundaries	**46**
Opt out of consumer culture wherever possible. Make, repair or swap things	**47**
Choose an alternative health practitioner and a mercury-free dentist	**48**
Cut down your mobile phone use, and don't allow children to use them	**49**
Hug a tree!	**50**

Green parenting

8

Contacts and resources

Green parenting

USEFUL CONTACTS

Pregnancy and Birth

Active Birth Centre
Workshops and yoga classes, baby massage classes, information and birthing pool hire.
020 7281 6760
www.activebirthcentre.com

Association of Radical Midwives
01695 572776

Association for Post-natal Illness
020 7386 0868

BLISS for parents of premature babies
0500 618140
www.bliss.org.uk

Doula Association
Birth support
www.doula.org.uk

Foresight
Pre-conceptual care
01483 868001

Home birth
www.homebirth.org.uk

Maternity Alliance
Info on maternity care, rights and benefits
020 7588 8582

Miscarriage Association
01924 200799

National Childbirth Trust
Antenatal classes and information
0870 444 8707
www.nctpregnancyandbabycare.com

Information on water birth
Gentlewater
www.gentlewater.co.uk

Twins and Multiple Births Association
0870 121 4000

Natural Babies

Association of Breastfeeding Mothers
Information and advice on breastfeeding
020 7813 1482
www.abm.me.uk

Breastfeeding Network
0870 9008787
www.breastfeeding.co.uk/bfn

CRY-SYS
Support for families with crying babies
020 7404 5011

Contacts and resources

La Leche League
Breastfeeding information and support
0845 120 2918
www.lalecheleague.org

National Association of Nappy Services
0121 693 4949

Real Nappy Association
020 8299 4519

UNICEF Baby Friendly Initiative
Info on breastfeeding, co-sleeping and more
www.babyfriendly.org.uk

Food and Nutrition

The Food Commission
020 7837 2250

National Association of Farmers Markets
01225 787914

Soil Association
0117 929 0661
www.whyorganic.org.uk

Sustain
020 7837 1228

Vegan Society
01424 427393

Vegetarian Society
0161 928 0793

Holistic Health

The Informed Parent
Information on vaccinations
020 8861 1022

National Asthma Campaign
0845 701 0203

National Autistic Society
020 8451 1114

National Eczema Society
020 7281 3553

Society of Homeopaths
01604 621400

Vaccination Awareness
0115 948 0829

Women's Nutrition Advisory Service
01273 487366

Natural Home

Centre for Alternative Technology
Information and advice on all aspects of green living including online shop and inspirational visitor centre
www.cat.org.uk
01654 705950

Garden Organic (HDRA)
www.gardenorganic.org.uk
024 7630 3517

Green parenting

National Recycling Forum
020 7253 6266

Wastewatch
www.wastewatch.org.uk

Green Issues

The Environment Trust
020 7377 0481

Friends of the Earth
020 7490 1555
www.foe.co.uk

Greenpeace
020 7865 8100
www.greenpeace.org.uk

Use Less Energy
www.uselessenergy.or.uk

Women's Environmental Network
020 7481 9004

General Parenting

Cleft Lip and Palate Association
020 7833 4883
www.clapa.com

Contact a Family
For families with special needs children
020 7383 3555

Exploring Parenthood
Parent's advice line
020 7221 6681

Family Line
0808 800 5678

The Green Parent Magazine
Bimonthly magazine about raising a family naturally.
www.thegreenparent.co.uk

National Meet-a-Mum Association
Puts mums in touch with other mothers locally
020 8768 0123

NSPCC
National Society for the Prevention of Cruelty to Children
0800 800 500

Parentline Plus
Helpline for parents and carers
0808 800 2222

Parent Network
020 7735 1214

Relate
Relationship counselling service
01788 573241

Stillbirth and Neonatal Death Society
Info and support groups for bereaved parents
020 7436 5881

Contacts and resources

SOURCE BOOK

21st Century Health
Products for a natural holistic home
www.21stcenturyhealth.co.uk

Arujo
Wooden fair trade toys
01295 271218
www.arujo.co.uk

Babykind
Good selection of cloth nappies of all shapes, sizes and colours
01286 882617
www.babykind.co.uk

Barefoot Books
Beautiful multicultural books for children
www.barefootbooks.co.uk

Barefoot Herbs
Herbal remedies for every stage of parenting
01273 480124
www.barefootherbs.co.uk

Bishopston Trading
Beautiful fair trade organic clothing for children and adults
0117 924 5598
www.bishopstontrading.co.uk

BORN
Extensive range of products to support attachment parenting
0117 924 5080
www.borndirect.com

B Small
Book publishers with a great range of craft and activity books for children
www.bsmall.co.uk

Cut 4 Cloth
Clothing range specially designed for cloth nappy babes
01326 340956
www.cut4cloth.co.uk

Floris Books
A range of books on ecological and educational matters including children's books
www.florisbooks.co.uk

Gossypium
Range of soft organic cotton clothing for babies, children and adults.
01273 488221
www.gossypium.co.uk

Green Baby
Everything a naturally raised baby needs from bedroom furniture to bibs.
0870 240 6894
www.greenbaby.co.uk

Green parenting

Green Books
Books about green issues and environmentalism
www.greenbooks.co.uk

Greenfibres
Wide range of products for the natural home including coir mattresses and organic clothing.
0845 330 3440
www.greenfibres.com

Green People
Organic toiletries for the whole family
01444 401444
www.greenpeople.co.uk

The Green Shop
Books, solar-powered toys, eco-gadgets, natural paints and more
01452 770629
www.thegreenshop.co.uk

Hejhog
Range of natural baby goodies including toys and toiletries
0845 606 6487
www.hejhog.co.uk

Holz Toys
Wooden toys and games
0845 130 8697
www.holztoys.co.uk

In a Soapnut Shell
Eco-laundry alternatives
www.inasoapnutshell.com

Lavera
Natural beauty products and cosmetics
01557 870203
www.lavera.co.uk

Little Green Earthlets
Range of goods including Motherease cloth nappies and natural toiletries
0845 072 4462
www.earthlets.co.uk

Lollipop
Organic cotton nappies, toys and more
01736 799 512
www.teamlollipop.co.uk

Myriad Natural Toys
Beautiful selection of toys
01725 517085
www.myriadonline.co.uk

Natural Child
Range of goods including cotton nappies and gorgeous natural baby products
01242 620988
www.naturalchild.co.uk

Natural Nursery
Toys, clothes, nappies, natural toiletries and more
0845 890 1665
www.naturalnursery.co.uk

Contacts and resources

Natural Mat
Natural latex mattresses for children's and adult beds.
0207 985 0474
www.naturalmat.com

Neal's Yard Remedies
Range of herbal medicines and beauty products
01747 834634
www.nealsyardremedies.com

RE
Gorgeous goods for the natural home
08700 416 548
www.be-re.com

Schmidt Natural Clothing
Wide range of children's and adult's clothing and organic wool nappies
0845 345 0498
www.naturalclothing.co.uk

Speizia Organics
Gorgeous organic beauty products
0870 850 8851
www.spieziaorganics.com

Tattybumpkin
Funky fresh organic children's clothing
01732 812212
www.tattybumpkin.com

The Natural Store
Gorgeous goodies for ladies, gentlemen and little ones
01273 746781
www.thenaturalstore.co.uk

Weleda
Anthrosophic medicine, natural toiletries and beauty products
0115 944 8200
www.weleda.co.uk

Yummies
Toys, nappies and more for the natural baby
01273 738733
www.yummies.biz

Don't Miss Out..

PRODUCT REVIEWS • COMPETITIONS • TRIED AND TESTED

The Green Parent

ONLY £2.95

Raising Kids with Conscience

WELL READ
Stay informed with this vibrant parenting magazine

ORGANIC
Recipes, seasonal food, healthy eating

Go green
ETHICAL SHOPPING made easy with our regular MARKETPLACE

ESSENTIAL
The UK's leading green lifestyle magazine

FREE INSIDE EVERY ISSUE: Magazine for children with nature activities

Bumps, birth and beyond • alternative education • food and drink
house and garden • holistic health and much more

Subscribe for just £17.50 a year

Annual subscription includes 6 issues of this gorgeous magazine
Back issues available for £3 each

3 WAYS TO SUBSCRIBE:
- **By Phone:** 01273 401012
- **Online:** www.thegreenparent.co.uk
- **By Post:** The Green Parent, PO Box 104, Lewes, BN7 9AX

This green lifestyle magazine covers all aspects of family life, from bumps to birth and beyond. Each issue is filled with inspiration, insightful journalism, beautiful photography, competitions and more. Children receive their own pull-out magazine crammed with nature activities, games and stories. Available to buy from your local newsagent, supermarkets and health food stores or order your copy here today.

"I can't wait for the next issue"
"Brilliant – nothing else like it!"
"Only magazine I've read from cover to cover in years"

TRIAL ISSUE AVAILABLE FOR JUST £3 Why not try the current issue before you buy a subscription? Just send back the attached form:

Title   First Name   Surname

Address

                                                  Postcode

Tel   Email

I would like a trial copy (£3) of the current issue (Please tick)

I would like a year's subscription (£17.50) starting with the current issue (Please tick)

Card No:

Valid from   Expiry Date   Issue No. (Switch Only)

I enclose a cheque for   made payable to 'The Green Parent'

Fill in this form and send to: The Green Parent, PO Box 104, Lewes, BN7 9AX

Also available from Impact Publishing

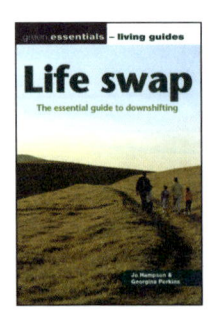

Life swap
– The essential guide to downshifting
Fed up with your current life? Spending too much and enjoying too little? Trapped in a stressful cycle of work and commitments? Life Swap shows you that there is an alternative – and if you care enough it is achievable. We give you the full low-down on the emotional and financial traps, the psychology for success, the money issues, work/life balance and the trick to changing your habits and expectations.
ISBN: 1 904601 43 X   £7.99

The toxic consumer
– How to reduce your exposure to everyday toxic chemicals
It is no longer controversial to claim that toxic chemicals are damaging our health. In this book we present the facts about what these chemicals can do and provide easy-to-follow practical advice on minimising your exposure and building up resistance.
ISBN: 1 904601 42 1   £7.99

Green Essentials
– organic gardening guides
Practical, fun and each one is focused on just one topic – making it the ideal way for busy gardeners or beginners to get all the top organic tips they need.

These books may be small but they're already making a big impression! And you know you can trust the organic advice they contain – all books carry the logos of the HDRA and the Soil Association.
£2.99 each

www.impactpublishing.co.uk